Literacy
AND THE
Youngest
Learner

Best Practices for Educators of Children from Birth to Five

V. Susan Bennett-Armistead • **Nell K. Duke** • **Annie M. Moses**

New York • Toronto • London • Auckland • Sydney
Mexico City • New Delhi • Hong Kong • Buenos Aires

Teaching Resources

Dedications

To my first and best teachers, my mom and dad. Thanks for reading to me even when you didn't have time, energy, or anything but love. —SBA

To teachers of young children everywhere—thank you. —NKD

To the teachers across the years who have fostered a love of learning and literacy in me, and especially to my family. —AM

CREDITS

PAGE 13: From *Madeline* by Ludwig Bemelmans, copyright 1939 by Ludwig Bemelmans, renewed © 1967 by Madeleine Bemelmans and Barbara Bemelmans Marciano. Used by permission of Viking Penguin, a Division of Penguin Young Readers Group, a Member of Penguin Group (USA) Inc., 345 Hudson Street, NY, NY 10014. All rights reserved.

PAGE 13: From *Too Many Rabbits and Other Fingerplays About Animals, Nature, Weather, and the Universe* by Kay Cooper. Text copyright © 1995 by Kay Cooper. Reprinted by permission of Scholastic Inc.

PAGE 13: From *Come Along, Daisy!* by Jane Simmons. Copyright © 1997 by Jane Simmons. Reprinted by permission of Orchard Books, UK, a division of The Watts Publishing Group Ltd., 96 Leonard Street, London, EC2A 4XD UK.

PAGES 16-17: Reprinted by permission from *Language Stories & Literacy Lessons* by Jerome C. Harste, Virginia A. Woodward, and Carolyn L. Burke. Copyright © 1984 by Jerome C. Harste, Virginia A. Woodward, and Carolyn L. Burke. Published by Heinemann, a division of Reed Elsevier, Inc., Portsmouth, NH. All rights reserved.

PAGES 19-21: Reprinted with permission from *Starting Out Right: A Guide to*

Promoting Children's Reading Success. Copyright © 1999 by the National Academy of Sciences, courtesy of the National Academies Press, Washington, DC.

PAGES 22-23: Reprinted by permission of International Reading Association. Copyright © 1988 by IRA and NAEYC. *Learning to Read and Write.* Washington, DC.

PAGE 64: From *Creepy Castle* by John S. Goodall. Copyright © 1975 by John S. Goodall, 1998 by the Estate of John S. Goodall. All rights reserved. Published by Macmillan Children's Books, UK.

PAGE 67: From *Eyes, Nose, Fingers, and Toes.* Text copyright © 1999 by Judy Hindley. Illustrations copyright © 1999 by Brita Granstrom. Reproduced by permission of the publisher Candlewick Press, Inc., Cambridge, MA, on behalf of Walker Books Ltd., London.

PAGE 79: From *On Reading Books to Children: Parents and Teachers* edited by Anne van Kleeck, Steven A. Stahl, and Eurydice B. Bauer. Copyright © 2003. Reprinted by permission of Lawrence J. Erlbaum Associates, Inc.

PAGE 81: From *Literacy Development in the Early Years: Helping Children Read and Write* by Lesley Mandel Morrow, © 1989, published by Allyn and Bacon, Boston, MA. Copyright © 1989 by Pearson Education. Reprinted by permission of the publisher.

PAGE 98: From *Is Your Mama a Llama?* by Deborah Guarino. Text copyright © 1989 by Deborah Guarino. Reprinted by permission of Scholastic Inc.

PAGE 99: From *Six Sick Sheep: 101 Tongue Twisters* by Joanna Cole and Stephanie Calmenson. Text copyright © 1993 by Joanna Cole. Used by permission of HarperCollins Publishers.

PAGE 189: From *Alphabet City* by Stephen T. Johnson, copyright © 1995 by Stephen T. Johnson. Used by permission of Viking Kestrel, a Division of Penguin Young Readers Group, a Member of Penguin Group, (USA) Inc., 345 Hudson Street, NY, NY 10014. All rights reserved.

PAGE 196: From *The Jolly Postman* by Allan Ahlberg. Copyright © 1986 by Allan and Janet Ahlberg. Used by permission of Little, Brown and Co., Inc.

PAGE 218: Clifford materials used with permission of Scholastic Inc.

Every effort has been made to find the authors and publishers of previously published material in this book and to obtain permission to print it. Every effort has also been made to find the photographers whose work appears in this book and credit them appropriately.

Cover and interior design by Maria Lilja
Cover photo: © Tim Hall/Photodisc Green/Getty Images
Interior photos by Shannon Poynter unless otherwise noted

ISBN 0-439-71447-8

1 2 3 4 5 6 7 8 9 10   23   11 10 09 08 07 06 05

Contents

Acknowledgments

When Nell and I finished our first book, we made a pact to never do it again. Anyone that has ever written a book knows it takes an enormous amount of energy and brainwork. It can be draining.

Obviously, we didn't keep our pact. We looked around at all the wonderful teachers that we've met and realized that many of them had the same questions about early literacy and that they needed support in the very valuable work that they do. So we embarked, this time with Annie Moses, on yet another exciting journey toward the completion of this book.

We were very fortunate to have so many skilled and willing helpers to create this book.

Nell would like to thank Michelle Allen for helping her identify children's books for several sections of this book, and Yonghan Park for assistance in tracking down references.

We all thank Sheila Bennett for her tireless reference hunting and editing.

Many images in the book come from a videotape developed by Nell Duke, Annie Moses, Alison Billman, Shenglan Zhang, and Susan Bennett-Armistead. We thank those who developed the videotape, especially the video editor Shenglan Zhang. We also thank the partners in the video development project—Michigan State University Families and Communities Together (FACT) coalition, in particular Patricia Farrell, Michigan Community Coordinated Child Care, in particular Norma Eppinger, and the Michigan Division of Day Care Licensing, in particular James Sinnamon.

We also thank the many teachers who shared their exemplary practice through stories and images both in the video and throughout this book. In particular, we thank Alison Billman, Nora Thompson, and the teachers of Michigan State University's Child Development Laboratories for their extra contributions to both the images and our thinking about the practices discussed in this book.

Neither Nell nor I would have written this book were we not assured that we would again have the chance to work with our editor, Ray Coutu. Ray is the best kind of editor. He possesses a solid understanding of young children and literacy, and is also a skilled writer himself. Even corrective feedback is positive and generally easy to swallow. His gentle guidance throughout the project has made this book what you hold in your hands. We simply could not have created the same book without him. Thank you, Ray.

Finally, we thank our families for their tireless and optimistic support of our work. The husbands, Dave Armistead (mine), Dave Ammer (Nell's), and Chris Consolati (Annie's) cared for children, made dinner (or at least ordered it in) and rubbed necks as needed. Our children, Julia (Nell's), Tim, Dawson, Violet, and Ababu (all mine) provided some of the images and much of the inspiration for this book. Thank you all for your patience, understanding, and love. We are so thankful that you understand that we want for all children what we have given our own, an early and enduring love of literacy.

V. Susan Bennett-Armistead

Foreword

Science proceeds by hypothesizing explanations, testing them, and eliminating the bad ones. Phlogiston, the four humors, and the revolution of the sun around the earth were all scientific hypotheses that, after lengthy struggles, were ultimately rejected and replaced by better ideas. In the field of early childhood literacy, readiness has been one of those bad but persistent ideas. Readiness is the idea that children should not be exposed to literacy prematurely, that they should display certain prerequisite maturational accomplishments (for example, clear hand preference, consistent directionality when writing, balance) before being asked to learn about letters and sounds. Readiness, as well as the associated notion that literacy depends on skills that mature (rather than on skills that are nurtured), has been shown to be incorrect. *Literacy and the Youngest Learner*, an extremely valuable, highly usable, and well-researched volume, should convince any lingering readiness-advocate that the time to replace the notion of readiness with a focus on literacy-rich early childhood environments has arrived.

Like persistent incorrect ideas in other fields, the notion of readiness served a purpose. At a time when literacy instruction was largely code-oriented, when worksheets were ubiquitous in first-grade classrooms, and when writing instruction guided children systematically, sequentially, and slowly from words to sentences to paragraphs to longer texts, the readiness notion protected preschool-age children from exposure to such practices, which might well have discouraged many from learning to read. But we now recognize that initial literacy instruction, in kindergarten through grade three, needs to integrate attention to the code with attention to meaning, and that fostering children's attention to literacy, motivation, and enjoyment of literacy is just as important as teaching them the alphabetic principle. And we now also understand that learning to read represents the weaving together of multiple skills, understandings, and orientations, many of which have their developmental origins in infancy and toddlerhood. Quite simply, children who have had richer literacy environments early on have developed those skills, understandings, and orientations further and are less likely to have difficulties with formal reading instruction in the primary grades.

In literate homes, children are exposed to and engaged in literacy practices—hearing bedtime stories, "writing" thank-you notes, making shopping lists, and discussing items in the morning paper—from birth onwards. Some early childhood settings, though, are literacy impoverished, whether because of a teacher's commitment to focusing on social and motor development (both worthy goals that are in no way in conflict with supporting literacy), because of a lack of books and other literacy resources, because the staff have little preparation in literacy, or because of a lingering belief in readiness. *Literacy and the Youngest Learner* will be instrumental in turning around these circumstances. Its readers will learn how to infuse literacy into the early childhood classroom in a way that is playful and motivating, how to overcome limitations in resources and in preparation, and, most important, how to confront the readiness argument with research. Every early childhood setting needs a copy of this book. Ideally, every early childhood educator would have a copy, and would use it as a text for self-guided or small-group professional development.

Catherine E. Snow, Harvard Graduate School of Education

Introduction

Literacy and the Youngest Learner is for people who believe—or who might be convinced—that literacy begins at birth. Intended for early childhood educators, including child-care providers, teachers, administrators, and curriculum developers, this book explains how to set infants (ages 0–1), toddlers (ages 1–3), and preschoolers (ages 3–5) on a course for lifelong interest and success in literacy. (Although we don't address kindergartners directly, many of the ideas we present can be applied to them.) Throughout the book we use the term *teacher* rather than *caregiver* or *child-care provider* because you teach children so much every day about themselves, the world around them, the people around them, and, we hope, literacy.

Photo: Alison Billman

How to Use This Book

This book can be read from cover to cover, in its entirety. Or you may choose to read chapters out of sequence, based on your needs and interests. For example, if you have been thinking about how to build literacy into your field trips, you might read chapter 10 first. The book can also be read "on the fly" by consulting the index or perusing the photographs and children's work throughout. We are sure you will find value in *Literacy and the Youngest Learner* no matter how you use it.

However you choose to read the book, your experience will be richer if you try out the ideas in early childhood environments, whether it's a child-care center, a small home day-care setting, a Head Start or Montessori pre-school—wherever professionals care for young children. From there, talk about the experience with colleagues, go back and refine your practice based on your discussions, and continue to share. The boxes on pages 8 and 9 provide advice related to a professional book club.

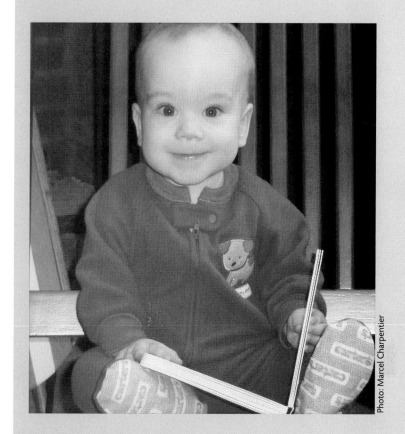

Photo: Marcel Charpentier

Even for Infants?!

It may be clear why we address preschoolers and toddlers, but infants? As a matter of fact, we have evidence that infants can engage in literacy activity. For example, Nell's daughter turned the pages of the board book *Do Monkeys Tweet?* (Walsh, 1997) at 3 months, and laughed at parts of Eric Carle's *The Very Busy Spider* (1984) at 6 months—and she has a videotape to prove it. Indeed, by the end of infancy, children growing up in literacy-rich homes can pretend to read books, make letterlike marks (in finger paint perhaps), and, most important, show a strong interest in reading and writing materials. Therefore, through-out the book, we discuss developmentally appropriate literacy-rich environments and activities for infants. Although there is little research on infants and print literacy (though much on infants and oral language, which underlies literacy), we believe more will be conducted as we come to understand how we lay foundations for literacy in our very youngest learners.

A Professional Book Club: Getting It Going, Keeping It Going

Getting together with colleagues to learn with one another around a professional book can be motivating and enriching. However, with so many demands on us it is hard to find time to plan and maintain book clubs. So when we do, we want them to be successful. Here is some advice:

Think carefully about the size of the book club.

Include enough people to make the discussion rich and varied, but not so many that it is hard for everyone to participate or find a time to meet (Roberts, 2003). We have found that groups of four to five work well.

Create a diverse group.

By including educators who work with different age groups, you encourage a developmental perspective and common principles. You may also want to include educators from different types of early childhood settings, for example from both a publicly funded and a tuition-based preschool or from a large commercial day-care center and a small home day-care setting. You may also want to include administrators. By doing so, you may generate ideas that lead to policy changes or materials purchases.

Set shared goals early on.

What do we want to get out of this club? What reading and other experiences are we planning? What do we expect from one another and ourselves? What would be signs of success? These are important questions to address early and to revisit regularly so that everyone is "on the same page" and satisfied with the book club (Roberts, 2003).

Hear from everyone.

Presumably, everyone has some expertise to bring to the book club because everyone has read the book or book chapter and has a response to share. Whether a member has been teaching for 1 year or 31 years, her thoughts matter. So do what you can to encourage everyone's participation right from the start.

Make connections to practice.

Book club discussions will be more powerful when you bring in your experiences: Perhaps a passage from the book made you think of something you heard a child say or maybe it made you think of an activity you sometimes do. The discussions will also be more powerful when you take what you are learning back to your room. Try looking at children's work in light of the discussion. Think about what was read and said. Experiment.

Book clubs provide a meaningful way for reading about and reflecting on our practice.

Six Ways to Use This Book in a Professional Book Club

Try one of the following activities after reading and discussing a chapter from this book, or try several activities after reading the entire book. Do whatever works best for your group and helps it reach its goals.

1 Child Study Select one child in your room and study his or her literacy closely for one week. What literacy or literacy-related interests does this child exhibit? What literacy-related knowledge does this child hold? Share your findings with the book club, supporting them with artifacts from the child, such as his or her writing or drawing.

2 Room or Building Inventory Take an inventory of the quantity and quality of print in your room. (See chapters 2 and 7 for ideas on what to look for.) What are its strengths? What are its weaknesses? Share your analysis with the club. Build on one another's strengths. After you have analyzed individual rooms, look at the whole building. How are hallways used? Common bathrooms? The office or waiting area? Consider using your book club as a task force for analyzing your total literacy program.

3 New Activity Try a new activity described in this book, or improve on an existing activity. Ask other members of your book club to observe you carrying out the activity, or arrange to be videotaped and screen the tape at the meeting. Discuss your strengths and weaknesses.

4 Materials Share Devote the first few minutes of each meeting to sharing literacy-related materials such as a particularly good children's book or a writing instrument children love. Consider swapping dramatic play props (see chapter 6), flannel board figures (see chapter 9), take-home bags (see chapter 12), or other materials that lend themselves to being used temporarily.

5 Co-planning Work together to plan a unit, lesson, field trip, family literacy workshop, or other event, drawing on what you learn from this book. Whether or not you and other club members teach together, co-planning can enhance everyone's practice.

6 Co-presenting Once your book club is up and running, and members have learned a critical amount, share the wealth by giving a presentation or poster session at a local, state, or national conference, or by arranging your own event.

Thank you for all you do for children. You play a critical role in laying the foundation for their literacy and our society. Together we can bring the power and joy of reading and writing to all children. We hope *Literacy and the Youngest Learner* will help you meet that important goal.

CHAPTER 1

The Importance of Literacy-Rich Activities and Environments for Young Children

Think about the role print has played in your day thus far. Perhaps you read a newspaper this morning at breakfast, scanned the nutrition information on a cereal box, left a note for a family member, paid the phone bill, reread a postcard on the refrigerator, followed signs on the way to work, checked a calendar. . . . Print is all around you. Reading and writing are integral to living well in our society.

Despite this fact, many infant, toddler, and preschool settings are devoid of literacy activities and materials. We have visited countless child-care centers, home-based facilities, and public and private preschools with little or no print on the walls, settings in which children are rarely given opportunities to hear text read to them, to draw and write, or to engage in other print-based activities (Duke, Moses, Subedi, Billman, & Zhang, 2005). This simply does not serve young children well.

This book is about why print-rich environments and activities are important for young children and how to provide them. In this chapter, we present several arguments for providing such environments and activities and explain how literacy for young children can be developmentally appropriate. In the chapters that follow, we show you how to apply these principles to your teaching every day.

Why Start So Early With Literacy?

Why is it so important to provide literacy-rich environments and activities for young children? Why should we put them on the road to reading and writing as early as infancy? Here are five good reasons, although there are undoubtedly many more.

Literacy Can Serve Many Purposes in Early Childhood Environments

Just as print plays an integral role in society, it can play an integral role in early childhood settings as well. For example, name tags can identify children's clothing, cubbies, and work. Labels and pictures can indicate where materials and toys are stored. Lists of favorite songs or games can serve as helpful reminders to teachers during the day. Daily Read Alouds can be engaging for children— just as engaging as dressing up, building with blocks, or playing on a jungle gym. Literacy is so intertwined in the environment and activities of many of the programs featured in this book that it is impossible to imagine what those programs would be like without it.

Literacy Can Be a Source of Great Joy for Young Children

For generations children have enjoyed wonderful books such as *The Snowy Day* by Ezra Jack Keats (1962), *The Runaway Bunny* by Margaret Wise Brown (1942), first-word books, counting books, texture books, and many others. We have never met a preschooler who did not respond with glee to the playful book *Tumble Bumble* by Felicia Bond (1996). We have never met an infant who was not captivated by Margaret Miller's *Baby Faces* (1998). Many adults can still tell you their favorite children's book. In fact, certain children's authors, such as Dr. Seuss and Maurice Sendak, conjure up so much nostalgia they have become a permanent part of adult popular culture. All children have a right to the joy that books and beloved authors can bring.

Literacy Provides a Way for Children to Learn About the World Around Them

Books and other print materials can help children explore and come to understand better the people, places, and things they encounter in everyday life. They can also help children learn about the world beyond their own. Children who live on a farm in Iowa can learn about people who live near the ocean in California. Children who live in the United States can learn about the history and culture of people from China. Children everywhere can learn about dinosaurs, the moon, and life underground. Literacy, like nothing else, puts the whole world in their hands.

Literacy Knowledge Is an Excellent Predictor of Children's Later School Achievement

Children who know alphabet letters and the sounds they represent, who can hear sounds in words, and who can understand how print works are far more likely to be good readers in kindergarten and in the grades that follow. (See Snow, Burns, & Griffin, 1998, for a review.) There is good reason to believe this connection is not just a coincidence but causal. Providing children strong literacy education in the early years has been shown to lead to better outcomes later on (Campbell, Ramey, Pungello, Sparling, & Miller-Johnson, 2002; Gray, Ramsey, & Klaus, 1982; Schweinhart, Barnes, & Weikart, 1993).

Literacy Builds Language Knowledge

Building children's vocabulary is a priority for most teachers, as it should be. However, unless children are exposed to books and other print materials, they may never encounter many words and complex structures that make up our language. Everyday oral language simply does not contain all those words and structures. Consider the following passages from children's books:

> **Tiptoeing with solemn face,**
> **with some flowers and a vase,**
> **in they walked and then said, "Ahhh,"**
> **when they saw the toys and candy**
> **and the dollhouse from Papa.**
>
> From *Madeline* by Ludwig Bemelmans

> **Something big stirred underneath her. Daisy shivered.**
> **She scrambled up onto the riverbank. Then something**
> **screeched in the sky above!**
>
> From *Come Along, Daisy!* by Jane Simmons

> **Bears find shelter during the cold winter months. Black**
> **bears stay in caves or in holes underneath the roots of fallen**
> **trees. Brown bears dig holes for themselves, while polar**
> **bears hollow out snowbanks.**
>
> From *Too Many Rabbits and Other Fingerplays About Animals, Nature, Weather, and the Universe* by Kay Cooper

"Providing children strong literacy education in the early years has been shown to lead to better outcomes later on (Campbell et. al., 2002; Gray et al., 1982; Schweinhart et al., 1993)."

These books, each appropriate even for toddlers, have rich vocabulary and sentence constructions. Hearing books like these helps children develop powerful and sophisticated language that can be important to their own writing and other forms of communication in later schooling, in their careers, and in their daily interactions (Senechal & LeFevre, 2002; Vivas, 1996; Whitehurst, Arnold, et al., 1994; Whitehurst, Epstein, et al., 1994).

The arguments for weaving literacy into young children's environments and activities are multiple and strong. However, some educators worry that it is not developmentally appropriate. As you might guess, we disagree. In the next section, we explain why.

Is Weaving Literacy Into Early Childhood Education Developmentally Appropriate for Young Children?

Some literacy activities are, indeed, not appropriate for our youngest learners: 40-page books for infants, hour-long Read Alouds for toddlers, flash cards for 3-year-olds, worksheets for 4-year-olds. (Sadly, these are all things we have seen being used in early childhood settings.) But literacy instruction can be developmentally appropriate. In fact, in 1998 the International Reading Association (IRA) and the National Association for the Education of Young Children (NAEYC) released a joint position statement on developmentally appropriate practice in literacy for young children. Important points in that statement, which was based on research, theory, and the perspectives of many experts in the field, include the following:

- "Children take their first critical steps toward learning to read and write very early in life."

- "Failing to give children literacy experiences until they are in school can severely limit the reading and writing levels they ultimately attain."

- "Recognizing the early beginnings of literacy acquisition too often has resulted in use of inappropriate teaching practices suited to older children or adults perhaps but ineffective with children in preschool, kindergarten, and the early grades."

At the same time:

- "The ability to read and write does not develop naturally, without careful planning and instruction."

(See Neuman, Copple, & Bredekamp, 2000, for the complete statement.)

A recent statement reinforces the earlier one and goes a step further by calling for all 3- and 4-year-old children to have access to free, high-quality public preschool that includes appropriate literacy experiences (International Reading Association, 2005). For more information on the statement update, go to http://www.reading.org. Other reviews of research, such as the report *Preventing Reading Difficulties,* produced by the National Research Council (Snow et al., 1998), and preliminary reports of the National Early Literacy Panel (Shanahan, Lonigan, Strickland, & Westburg, 2004) also take the strong position that literacy should have a significant place in the lives of children from birth to age 5. The issue is not whether to weave literacy into early childhood environments and activities, but how to do so in ways that are developmentally appropriate and productive. This book helps show you how.

Literacy Development Begins at Birth

Educators used to believe there was a particular age when children were "ready to read." One study, published in 1931, even determined this magic age to be 6.5 years (Morphett & Washburne, 1931; see response from Gates, 1937). But more recent thinking says that literacy "emerges" from birth, assuming the child is being raised in a literate world. Long before children can read and write in the conventional sense, they are learning about literacy (Clay, 1972; Teale & Sulzby, 1986a; Whitehurst & Lonigan, 2001). Specifically, they are learning the following:

Why People Read

A trip to the grocery store helps children see the use of literacy to label (as on food products and sections of the store), to advertise (as in the weekly circular), to inform (as with nutrition information on the products), to entitle (as with coupons), to remember (as with a shopping list), and so on. There are many reasons people read and write and many purposes for reading and writing. As children see people read and write, and participate in reading and writing activities, they learn about some of these purposes.

Developing Literacy *Is* Part of Developing the Whole Child

Early childhood educators often talk of developing "the whole child," meaning we should address all important areas of growth, including cognitive, physical, socio-emotional, linguistic, creative, and others, not just a few. However, literacy has traditionally taken a backseat to these areas and, at times, hasn't even been considered. In fact, the NAEYC's statement on developmentally appropriate practice (1997) gave only a passing nod to literacy development. Much more space was dedicated to discussing social and emotional development.

A growing number of early childhood educators have a different view. We believe that literacy development is a fundamental area of development— one that is essential to developing the whole child. Of course, we do not want to see a focus on literacy detract from developing children in other areas. At the same time, we do not want to see literacy neglected. As educators and people who care for and about young children, we have an obligation to develop children's literacy skills and understandings along with other aspects of their developing selves.

What People Read

Many children are cognizant of the different types of things we read. One of our favorite examples comes from a 3-year-old child who scribble-wrote two texts—one with short scribbles in a narrow column down one side of the page, another with long scribbles that extended across the page. She identified the former as a shopping list and the latter as a story! Already she knew something about these two different kinds of text. (See figure 1.1.)

How People Read

Many young children, even in their infancy, begin to learn about how we read. In other words, they develop concepts of print, alphabet knowledge, and the ability to comprehend written language. For example, they learn that

- we read (English) from left to right and top to bottom.

- we read words, as opposed to making a story up or reading just the pictures on a page.

- we identify words by looking at their letters, which in turn represent sounds in speech.

- we use different parts of the text—such as words, illustrations, graphs, and the context of reading—to help us make meaning.

(For further discussion of children's growing knowledge about reading, see chapter 2.)

FIGURE 1.1
Hannah, age 3, writes a shopping list and a story.

BIRTHDAY LIST   **MAP**   **LETTER**   **STORY PAGE**

FIGURE 1.2
Stephanie writes a birthday list, map, letter, and story page just before entering first grade.

So often people think about young children as prereaders or nonreaders and don't pay much attention to their early interactions with print. But if people ignore what children already know about literacy, they'll miss an important opportunity to build on that knowledge. The same goes for writing. For some time, researchers have been doing just that, looking at children's early attempts at composing, and getting fascinating results (Ferreiro & Teberosky, 1982; Harste, Woodward, & Burke, 1984; Sulzby, 1986). Consider the example in figure 1.2. This 5-year-old child has learned so much about literacy. She has learned that we use print to keep track of things (birthday list), inform (map), communicate (letter), and entertain (story page). She has learned that we use letters in written language, has learned many sound-letter relationships (for example, the letter *m* for the sound /m/), and has even learned the conventional spellings for some words (for example, Love, her name). She knows that we use spaces to separate words, that we write and read from left to right and top to bottom. She knows that a list is usually a single column of words or phrases on a common topic, that a letter often begins with a salutation (Dear Mom), ends with a closing statement (Love Steph), and contains a personal message. She even knows that we often use decorative stationery for letters! She knows that a map tells us how to get

> **❝** *There is no magic time when children 'are readers and writers.' Children are always becoming readers and writers.* **❞**

Emergent Literacy Defined

Emergent literacy refers to the point in children's development before they are conventionally literate—that is, before they can read on their own or write text that others can read (Clay, 1966, as cited in Teale & Sulzby, 1986b). Unlike "reading readiness," emergent literacy assumes that literacy learning begins from birth and emerges gradually over time. There is no magic time when children "are readers and writers." Children are always becoming readers and writers. They are born ready to learn about literacy and continue to grow in their literacy understandings throughout life. The concept is important to all of us as early childhood educators because it implies that work we do around children's literacy development is critical and consequential. The magic age is now.

to or to find places and that, in a map, words are intermingled with graphics. In contrast, on her story page, she separates the words and the graphics, but maintains a thematic relationship, as story writers often do. And this analysis doesn't cover all this child knows about literacy! Indeed, research indicates that young children of different economic, racial, ethnic, and language backgrounds all learn a great deal about literacy when they are exposed to it (Purcell-Gates, 1996; Taylor & Dorsey-Gaines, 1988).

What Are Expectations for Literacy Learning, Birth to 5?

If we agree that literacy emerges from birth, a next logical question is, what should we expect from children at different ages? What should children know and be able to do in literacy when they leave toddlerhood and enter preschool? How about by the end of the preschool years? Having answers may help you to develop appropriate environments and activities for the age group with which you are working (as will this whole book, we hope).

Goals for Birth to 3-Year-Old, 3- to 4-Year-Old, and Kindergarten According to the NRC

Increasingly, in part as a result of the No Child Left Behind Act (2001) and other government initiatives in early childhood education, state, county, and district education agencies have developed typical accomplishments for children when they reach specific ages. You should look for any that apply to your area because you may be held accountable to those by parents or licensors. There have also been a few national attempts to develop expectations. One, which we share here, is from *Starting Out Right: A Guide to Promoting Children's Reading Success* by the National Research Council, edited by M. Susan Burns, Peg Griffin, and Catherine E. Snow, (1999), which was written as a follow-up for teachers and parents to *Preventing Reading Difficulties in Young Children* report (Snow et al., 1998).

Like developmental milestones in any area, literacy accomplishments will vary from child to child and depend on the experiences each child has had. A child who comes to you at age 3 having been read to very little at home or in previous care settings may not meet these expectations. A child who has been provided with literacy-rich activities and environments from birth is likely to exceed them. For all of the children in our care we view what follows as minimum expectations.

Birth to Three-Year-Old Accomplishments

- Recognizes specific books by cover.
- Pretends to read books.
- Understands that books are handled in particular ways.
- Enters into a book-sharing routine with primary caregivers.
- Vocalization play in crib gives way to enjoyment of rhyming language, nonsense word play, etc.

- Labels objects in books.
- Comments on characters in books.
- Looks at picture in book and realizes it is a symbol for real object.
- Listens to stories.
- Requests/commands adult to read or write.
- May begin attending to specific print, such as letters in names.

- Uses increasingly purposeful scribbling.
- Occasionally seems to distinguish between drawing and writing.
- Produces some letter-like forms and scribbles with some features of English writing.

  (Burns et al., 1999, p. 59)

Three- to Four-Year-Old Accomplishments

- Knows that alphabet letters are a special category of visual graphics that can be individually named.

- Recognizes print in the local environment.

- Knows that it is the print that is read in stories.

- Understands that different text forms are used for different functions of print (e.g., a list for groceries is different than the list on a menu).

- Pays attention to separable and repeating sounds in language (e.g., in Peter, Peter, Pumpkin Eater: Peter Eater).

- Uses new vocabulary and grammatical constructions in own speech.

- Understands and follows oral directions.

- Is sensitive to some sequences of events in stories.

- Shows an interest in books and reading.

- When being read a story, connects information and events to real-life experiences.

- Questions and comments demonstrate understanding of literal meaning of story being told.

- Displays reading and writing attempts, calling attention to self: "Look at my story."

- Can identify about 10 alphabet letters, especially those from own name.

- Writes (scribbles) message as part of playful activity.

- May begin to attend to beginning or rhyming sounds in salient words.

    (Burns et al., 1999, p. 59)

Kindergarten Accomplishments

- Knows the parts of a book and their functions.

- Begins to track print when listening to a familiar text being read or when rereading own writing.

- "Reads" familiar texts emergently, i.e., not necessarily verbatim from the print alone.

- Recognizes and can name all uppercase and lowercase letters.

- Understands that the sequence of letters in a written word represents the sequence of sounds (phonemes) in a spoken word (alphabetic principle).

- Learns many, though not all, one-to-one letter-sound correspondences.

- Recognizes some words by sight, including a few very common ones ("the," "I," "my," "you," "is," "are").

- Uses new vocabulary and grammatical constructions in own speech.

- Makes appropriate switches from oral to written language styles.

- Notices when simple sentences fail to make sense.

- Connects information and events in texts to life and life experiences to text.

- Retells, reenacts, or dramatizes stories or parts of stories.

- Listens attentively to books the teacher reads to class.

- Can name some book titles and authors.

- Demonstrates familiarity with a number of types or genres of text (e.g., storybooks, expository texts, poems, newspapers, and everyday print such as signs, notices, labels).

- Correctly answers questions about stories read aloud.

- Makes predictions based on illustrations or portions of stories.

- Demonstrates understanding that spoken words consist of sequences of phonemes.

- Given spoken sets like "dan, dan, den," can identify the first two as the same and the third as different.

- Given spoken sets like "dak, pat, zen," can identify the first two as sharing one same sound.

- Given spoken segments, can merge them into a meaningful target word.

- Given a spoken word, can produce another word that rhymes with it.

- Independently writes many uppercase and lowercase letters.

- Uses phonemic awareness and letter knowledge to spell independently (invented or creative spelling).

- Writes (unconventionally) to express own meaning.

- Builds a repertoire of some conventionally spelled words.

- Shows awareness of distinction between "kid writing" and conventional orthography.

- Writes own name (first and last) and the first names of some friends or classmates.

- Can write most letters and some words when they are dictated.

(Burns et al., 1999, p. 85)

Photo: Pamela Green

Goals for Preschool and Kindergarten According to the IRA and NAEYC

A second set of expectations comes from the International Reading Association and the National Association for the Education of Young Children's joint position statement (1998), which we referred to earlier. It does not provide expectations for infants and toddlers, but does for preschoolers and kindergartners.

Goals for Preschool

Children explore their environment and build the foundations for learning to read and write.

CHILDREN CAN

- enjoy listening to and discussing storybooks
- understand that print carries a message
- engage in reading and writing attempts
- identify labels and signs in their environment
- participate in rhyming games
- identify some letters and make some letter-sound matches
- use known letters or approximations of letters to represent written language (especially meaningful words like their name and phrases such as "I love you")

WHAT TEACHERS DO

- share books with children, including Big Books, and model reading behaviors
- talk about letters by name and sounds
- establish a literacy-rich environment
- reread favorite stories
- engage children in language games
- promote literacy-related play activities
- encourage children to experiment with writing

WHAT PARENTS AND FAMILY MEMBERS CAN DO

- talk with children, engage them in conversation, give names of things, show interest in what the child says
- read and reread stories with predictable texts to children
- encourage children to recount experiences and describe ideas and events that are important to them
- visit the library regularly
- provide opportunities for children to draw and print, using markers, crayons, and pencils

Goals for Kindergarten

Children develop basic concepts of print and begin to engage in and experiment with reading and writing.

KINDERGARTNERS CAN

- enjoy being read to and themselves retell simple narrative stories or informational texts

- use descriptive language to explain and explore

- recognize letters and letter-sound matches

- show familiarity with rhyming and beginning sounds

- understand left-to-right and top-to-bottom orientation and familiar concepts of print

- match spoken words with written ones

- begin to write letters of the alphabet and some high-frequency words

WHAT TEACHERS DO

- encourage children to talk about reading and writing experiences

- provide many opportunities for children to explore and identify sound-symbol relationships in meaningful contexts

- help children to segment spoken words into individual sounds and blend the sounds into whole words (for example, by slowly writing a word and saying its sound)

- frequently read interesting and conceptually rich stories to children

- provide daily opportunities for children to write

- help children build a sight vocabulary

- create a literacy-rich environment for children to engage independently in reading and writing

WHAT PARENTS AND FAMILY MEMBERS CAN DO

- daily read and reread narrative and informational stories to children

- encourage children's attempts at reading and writing

- allow children to participate in activities that involve writing and reading (for example, cooking, making grocery lists)

- play games that involve specific directions (such as "Simon Says")

- have conversations with children during mealtimes and throughout the day

Note: This list is intended to be illustrative, not exhaustive. Children at any grade level will function at a variety of phases along the reading/writing continuum.

(IRA & NAEYC, 1998, p. 8)

Looking at long lists of expectations like this can be overwhelming. It can be frustrating, too, if you feel they include things that over- or underestimate what children should know and be able to do, or when they seem to contradict one another. (Maybe you noticed, the NRC document calls for "letter-like forms and scribbles" by age 3, whereas the IRA/NAEYC document calls for "known letters or approximations of letters" in preschool.) So it's important to view these lists as starting points for thinking through your own expectations. As you read this book, and reflect on your experiences, identify what you expect from infants, toddlers, and preschoolers, and compare them with what we expect. You will see that our expectations are high, but attainable with well-planned, appropriate, and responsive literacy environments and activities.

Concluding Thoughts

We hope this chapter has helped convince you, or affirmed your belief, that literacy development begins at birth, and that important literacy knowledge and skills emerge—depending on the quality of environments and activities—from birth. We hope that you believe, as we do, that it is important to focus on literacy in early childhood not just because it prepares children for later life, but because of the enjoyment and stimulation that literacy offers them now. In the next chapter, we discuss specific areas of early childhood literacy learning and our overall vision for how the environment you create can help children accomplish this learning. There are so many ways to build literacy in young children. Let's explore them!

Send Parents a Powerful Message About Literacy's Importance

When your entire day is packed with literacy experiences, you show parents that you value literacy and that you are committed to helping their children gain literacy skills through appropriately planned play experiences. You also model for parents a variety of experiences they can do at home with their children. For more ways of helping parents to promote literacy, see chapter 12.

Young Children Gain Literacy Regardless of the Activity They Choose

You may have a child who never leaves a particular classroom area given the opportunity. We had one who refused to leave the block area. Luring him to the book corner would take a miracle. But because literacy was woven throughout our classroom environment, he could stay in the block area and still be exposed to important literacy-building opportunities, including books on houses and construction vehicles, labels on the block shelves with shape names (square, small rectangle, large rectangle, triangle, wedge, etc.), and a clipboard and graph paper for documenting the buildings he created. All these activities reinforced what he was doing but also helped build a solid foundation of literacy. If every area and activity is connected to literacy, each child will have a chance to interact with it on his or her own terms and level of readiness.

Young Children Spend More Time Building Skills

As you will learn in the upcoming chapters, most large-group experiences last only a few minutes (as they should). We think children need more exposure to literacy than a single story at group time. Providing that exposure throughout the day ensures a rich literacy environment that supports children's literacy knowledge much better than just one three-minute Read Aloud can. More, in this case, really is better.

Finally, weaving literacy into the whole day is just plain fun for everyone! This approach has enriched not only the children's literacy lives but also the work of many teachers we know.

Provide a Literacy-Rich Classroom Environment

A literacy-focused classroom promotes interaction with text. To create such a classroom, you need to consider three things: the classroom library, print on walls and other surfaces, and materials that promote interaction with print and its purposes. In this section, we discuss each of those things.

The Classroom Library

Children need to interact with books to learn to love literacy and gain the skills necessary to be successful with it. With that in mind, the library should be considered the heart of a literacy-focused classroom. Neuman, Celano, Greco, and Shue (2001) recommend classrooms have approximately five to eight books per child. That would mean in a class of 18 children, its library should contain between 90 and 144 books. Does that mean all those books should be on display and available at all times? Not necessarily. We find that, if you rotate selections often, offering five to ten more books than the number of children in your class works well because it provides each child with one book plus some extra choices.

The library should contain wordless picture books, stories, informational books, rhyming texts, alphabet books, books based on songs, and stories about real people. Infants and toddlers need books that can be wiped clean, fiction board books, nonfiction board books, concept books that take on big topics like numbers, colors, feelings, and shapes such as *The Shape of Things* by Dayle Dodds (1996). Board books based on familiar songs, like *Baby Beluga* by Raffi (1997), are good choices, too, since many children are likely to know at least some of the words. See chapter 7 for many more suggestions for building your library.

In a literacy-enriched classroom, book display (top) and storage (bottom) are critical issues.

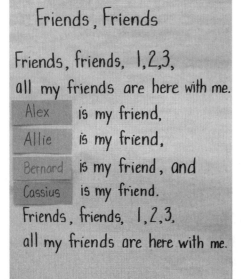

Friends, Friends

Friends, friends, 1,2,3,
all my friends are here with me.
Alex   is my friend,
Allie   is my friend,
Bernard is my friend, and
Cassius is my friend.
Friends, friends, 1,2,3,
all my friends are here with me.

Print on Walls and Other Surfaces

Researchers Lea McGee, Richard Lomax, and Martha Head (1988) and Susan Neuman and Kathleen Roskos (1993a) found that children learned a lot about reading when their environment included labels on materials, print on bulletin boards, and signs for activity centers and for use in play. By displaying informational posters, song charts, cartoons, and captioned pictures that promote a weekly theme, you can include more print in your environment.

One classroom we visited recently had a "floor book" for the infants. The teachers labeled photographs of the children and their families, put them on the floor, covered them with clear contact paper, and talked to infants about them throughout the day. Published books can be used in the same way by simply disassembling them and affixing them to the floor or a low surface. (You'll probably need two copies of the book so you can get both sides of the pages.)

A word of caution: Unless environmental print is changed regularly and referred to often, children ignore it like wallpaper, and if it is changed too frequently, children do not have time to master the texts present. A balance is needed. Text doesn't have meaning to children unless we point it out to them and rotate it carefully.

Top: *Simply writing out the lyrics to songs on chart paper can enrich your classroom's environmental print.*

Bottom: *This 9-month-old enjoys engaging independently with a "floor book" created by disassembling then laminating a favorite board book.*

Top left: *Labeling high-interest objects, like a fish tank, adds text to the classroom environment. The teacher who created this display asks, "How many fish do you see?"*

Top right: *Hallways are great places to display text. In this example, teachers use covers and pages from children's books.*

Bottom: *Children can locate their own coat hooks, lockers, and cubbies when their names are posted nearby.*

Target Important Areas of Literacy Development

Many of us who were trained to be teachers of young children were not trained in literacy development. Either we were in programs that didn't deem literacy as important for young children or we were trained at a time when attention to literacy was perceived to be developmentally inappropriate. (A teacher once asked Susan if it was okay to put an alphabet poster up in her room or if that would be "pushing" the 4-year-olds too much. Answer: Yes, include the poster!) Now we know better. Children whose early childhood education targets important areas of literacy development are more successful in literacy in primary settings (Campbell et al., 2002; Gray et al., 1982; Schweinhart et al., 1993). So, what are these areas of development? We see nine major ones, based on the literacy goals identified on pages 19–24. They are as follows:

Concepts of Print

The understanding of how books "work," such as that they have a front and a back, are read from left to right, have pictures that give us information about the text, have spaces separating words (concept of word), and have words that don't change between readings. (See chapter 4 for in-depth coverage of developing concepts of print.)

Phonological Awareness

The ability to hear differences and similarities in the sounds of words and parts of words. The awareness of individual sounds and groups of sounds in words, including the ability to separate words into syllables or beats; blend sounds into words; segment words into sounds; recognize and generate words with similar beginning, middle, and ending sounds; and move sounds around to make new words. (See chapter 5 for in-depth coverage of promoting phonological awareness.)

Alphabetic Principle

The notion that words are made up of letters, that the letters stand for the sounds we make when we say the words, and that by putting the letters together in various ways we make different words.

Letter-Sound Knowledge

Knowledge of the sound or sounds associated with each letter. (See chapter 4 for in-depth coverage of building letter-sound knowledge.)

Vocabulary

The collection of words we understand when reading and listening (receptive vocabulary) and/or use when writing and speaking (expressive vocabulary). (See chapter 3 for in-depth coverage of developing vocabulary.)

Oral Language

The understandings we have about how oral language is used to communicate as well as our understanding of word usage and placement within speech. (See chapter 3 for in-depth coverage of promoting oral language.)

Listening or Reading Comprehension

The ability to extract and construct meaning from/with text that is read aloud, or that one reads oneself. This requires language knowledge, world knowledge, comprehension strategies, and knowledge about text and genre. (See chapter 4 for in-depth coverage of building comprehension.)

Understandings of Genre

The understanding that text is used and created for different purposes and comes in different forms based on those purposes, such as newspapers, lists, stories, information books, and poems. (See chapter 7 for in-depth coverage of understanding genres.)

Motivation to Engage With Text

The desire to read, write, listen to, or otherwise interact with written language. Motivation is affected by a child's perception of the value of the activity (is this worthwhile? is this important?), the child's perception of himself (am I good at this? can I do this?), and other factors.

Photo: Kelly Rae Chapin

By putting novel materials in a writing center, teachers lure children in to try them.

chapters where that area is discussed. Or you can read whole chapters, such as "Dramatic Play and Literacy" (chapter 6), knowing that each area is addressed within it. Either way works. Think about what you know, what you want to know, and what makes sense for you and your children.

We're not asking you to change what you're doing completely. You will still have group time, gym time, outside time, and all the play centers that you have had in the past, but they will be literacy enhanced. This book will help you think about how to plan for literacy across and throughout your day. In the next chapter, you will learn the importance of creating a solid foundation in oral language as well as ways to support children's oral language development. Chapter 4 helps you make the most out of reading aloud to children. Chapter 5 shows you how to promote children's phonological awareness, a critical stepping stone to learning how to read and write. The rest of the book will help you think about literacy during specific times of your day and in specific areas of your room.

Our goal is to help you put literacy at the foundation of everything else you teach. The doctor's office in the dramatic play area might have writing materials in it; the art area might include alphabet-letter-shaped cookie cutters for stamping letters; the songs you sing might contain rhymes that help children isolate and distinguish the sounds within words; children might line up by the sound of the first letter in their names; the texture table might contain items that result in children learning new vocabulary like *sticky*, *gooey*, *smooth*, and *rough*; the stories you read

Sample Daily Plan (half day)
Weekly Theme: Marvelous Me!

Circle Time:

MUSIC: "Hello Song" (Use each child's name as you draw it out of a bag.)

STORY: "I Like Me"

DISCUSSION: Things we like about ourselves

GROUP DICTATION: Brainstorm something you like about yourself to include in group chart.

DISCUSSION: Options for choice time

Choice-Time Options:

ART: Body tracing with a friend. Cut out body shapes, decorate them, and label parts of the body. (Make sure there are several texts with names of body parts on them in the area.)

DRESS-UP: Baby Hospital. Dramatic play kit includes appointment book, anatomy texts, prescription pads, books about taking care of babies, paper, pencils, phone, posters with body parts on them, scale and record charts, as well as the usual doctor's office stuff.

CONSTRUCTION: Building Homes. Include photos of children's homes, dollhouse, people figures, books depicting homes around the world, books depicting construction of homes.

SCIENCE CORNER: Include interactive graph to document eye color, mirrors, Spier's book entitled *People*.

LISTENING CENTER: Include *I Like Me!* tape and set of books.

BOOK LOFT: Include books about self-esteem.

WRITING CENTER: Include stationery, pens, stampers, scissors, file box with names and pictures of all children in the class. Prompt: Write to someone you like, telling what you like about him or her. (Be sure to move the chart from circle time to the center to act as a word wall for the children.)

Pre-Snack Time:

Sing "Willoughby Wallaby Woo." Conduct snack survey: Pass out paper and pencils to the children and ask them to write whether they would like graham crackers or cheese crackers for snack. Total the responses and decide.

Handwashing/Bathroom/Snack:
Label baskets with the number of crackers per child.

Clean Up for Outside Time
(or Gym if it's rainy)

Outside Time/Gym:

Run to one anothers' names written in sidewalk chalk; engage in a scavenger hunt using written picture clues.

Dismissal

---

might start "once upon a time" and end with "happily ever after" and, therefore, teach an important lesson in story language. All of these experiences promote particular understandings that not only support literacy skills later, but also support them *right now*.

Purposeful planning ensures that we address all nine areas of literacy development—areas that are too important to leave to chance. Just as we would with any area of development, we must continuously assess where children are and in what ways they need support. That does not mean administering tests to young children. It *does* mean carefully monitoring their language use, their ability to retell stories, and the many ways they use and produce text. This helps us not only to keep track of where children are in their learning but to determine the direction of our planning. There should be no rigid, prescribed scope and

Susan worked in a mixed-age classroom that followed a "literacy link" approach, meaning that every center and activity had some connection to developing literacy skills. Literacy was at the foundation of her classroom and all tasks were anchored to it.

Weekly Overview Theme: Community			Lead Student Teacher: Ms. Finkbeiner Date: February 14-17	
Domain	Monday	Tuesday	Wednesday	Thursday
Aesthetics	Shaving cream play	Scarf dancing	Painting with rubber band brushes	Silly dance contest
Affective	Cleaning badge	Community portraits	Our classroom as a community	Class voting
Cognitive	Community puzzles	Computer	Creating rain	Needs vs. wants
Construction	Legos	Classroom newspaper	Classroom newspaper	Lincoln blocks
Language	Making letters out of play dough	Community clues	Matching letter with community object	Community journals
Physical	Follow the leader	Painting snow	Touring our school community	Head, shoulder, knees and toes.
Pretend Play	Dollhouse and apartment structure with dolls	-- Grocery	store --	
Social	Classroom rules	Large floor puzzle	How we help each other	Clean up after oneself
Large Group Focus	Creating classroom rules	Dancing with scarves	Our classroom school as a community	My perfect neighborhood
Parent	Cadigan Smith	Jack Sparrow		Kelly Wang

Laurie Linscott teaches 20 3- to 5-year-old children in a half-day program. Admittedly, her weekly plan, which was created by student teacher Caryn Finkbeiner, probably looks a great deal like any plan for preschool. The difference is the literacy component of each activity. You can see that many areas of development are addressed across the week. For example, the Lego area has signs to add to structures and the grocery store has containers that children can read.

sequence for teaching these areas of development. We need to provide a carefully planned and prepared buffet of literacy opportunities and monitor what children are taking in and how they are using it. For ideas on monitoring children's development, check out Sharon MacDonald's *The Portfolio and Its Use: A Road Map for Assessment* (1997) and Anne K. Soderman, Kara M. Gregory, and Louise T. McCarty's *Scaffolding Emergent Literacy: A Child-Centered Approach for Preschool Through Grade 5* (2005).

Concluding Thoughts

A print-rich environment and activities are part of the foundation of a literacy-focused classroom. The rest of the foundation is constructed from strong understandings of young children and literacy. By weaving literacy into your total program, you honor children's development and provide them with solid beginnings for literacy success. Let this book be a guide.

DOMAIN: Physical   AREA: Learning Centers (hallway)

ACTIVITY TITLE: Roller Racers
INTERMEDIATE OBJECTIVE: Children have opportunities to use their whole bodies in appropriate activities to strengthen muscles and muscle groups.

TFP'S (Terms, Facts, Principles):
- Children can use their legs and arms to move around on roller racers.
- Driving on roller racers and other vehicles can be fun, but we have to be careful.
- Drivers have to follow rules and signs, and cooperate to avoid crashes.
- Signs help drivers know what to do.

MATERIALS:
- Two roller racers or scooters
- Five orange cones
- Traffic signs: Go, Yield, and Stop
- Brown tape (starting point)

PROCEDURE:
1. Discuss with children that they will be driving a roller racer today.
2. Hold a brief discussion that incorporates the TFP's.
3. Explain to the children that they will be driving their roller racers in and out of orange cones, following the traffic signs along the way. (There are three: Go, Yield, and Stop.)
4. Place the orange cones about five feet apart in a straight line.
5. Put the Go sign in front, the Yield sign at the fourth cone, and Stop sign at the fifth cone.
6. Tell children that they will be weaving through the orange cones.
7. Check to make sure children understand the meaning of each traffic sign.
8. Let children drive their roller racer.
9. Talk about how rules and signs kept them from crashing.
10. Let children repeat this activity if there is no one waiting.

Literacy Link: Use the traffic signs, Go, Yield, and Stop.

HINTS for Success: Be sure that the children understand the traffic signs and know how to maneuver the roller racer through the orange cones.

EXTENSIONS: Have older or more experienced children go through the course multiple times. Challenge them by adding different traffic signs and extra cones.

SIMPLIFICATIONS: For younger or less experienced children, take two of the orange cones away to shorten the course. In addition, guide those who have limited upper-body strength by holding one of the handlebars, supporting them through the course.

This is an activity "card" created by Christopher Robinson, a teacher in an all-day class of 21 children aged 3 to 5, which might be used by a volunteer or assistant teacher. Each card shows the dual planning associated with the activity. On this card, for example, you'll notice that children are driving roller racers as well as learning about and reading signs.

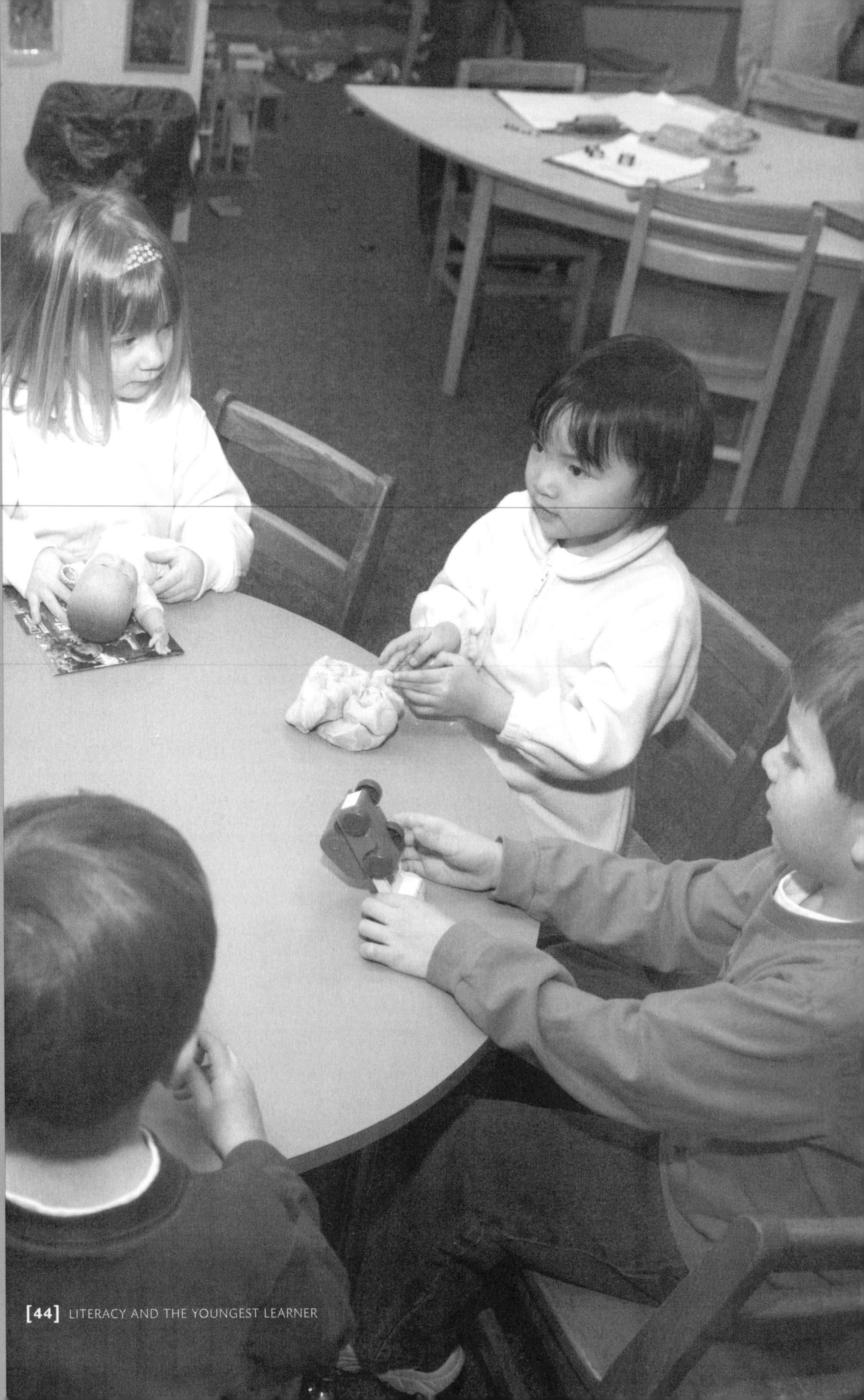

CHAPTER 3

Developing Oral Language

A child is playing teacher. She calls out, "Come here." "Quiet down."

"Look at me!" Another child is playing teacher. She says, "This is a giraffe.

It's a animal. Who can tell me about it?"

These two children have developed very different ideas of how a teacher talks. In this chapter we argue that teacher talk matters a lot to children's development. In fact, we argue that talk in general matters a lot. This is the only chapter that does not focus on reading and writing. Why? Because oral language is so important to reading and writing development, so important to a quality literacy environment, that it deserves a chapter.

Study after study shows relationships between children's language development and their literacy development (Scarborough, 2001; Snow, 1983). Children who have strong oral-language skills often have strong reading and writing skills. In contrast, children with oral-language problems are at higher risk of reading and writing difficulties (Scarborough). These close relationships between oral-language abilities and written-language abilities are not surprising in that both involve language. While oral and written language are not the same (see discussion in chapter 4), there are many points of overlap and similarities. This chapter is divided into two major sections. In the first section, we discuss strategies for promoting oral-language development. In the second, we discuss strategies to avoid— things *not to do*—when it comes to promoting oral language.

Strategies for Promoting Oral-Language Development

Early childhood educators can make a real difference in children's language development (Barnett, 2001; Dickinson & Sprague, 2001; McCartney, 1984). There are many things you can do every day:

Talk With Children Whenever and Wherever You Can

Few things are more important than conversing with children. Make this a priority every day. Seize every moment to talk about children's friends, their families, their favorite activities, their favorite foods, the outfit they're wearing—whatever. Just talk, regardless of the child's age or stage of language development.

When observing early childhood education environments, we have watched how much, and how little, educators talk with each child in their care. The result? In some settings some children go hours without being addressed. It's enough to break your heart—and to make us all work hard to ensure we spend time conversing with each child each day.

Get Close

In some instances, it's not about how much we say, but from where we say it. Avoid talking too far from children. Get up close so they can see your lips and facial expressions, hear your voice clearly, and make eye contact with you. This will make it more likely that they engage with what you are saying and learn from it.

Really Listen

We have all had the experience of talking to someone who is not really listening to us. How can we tell? Perhaps they are looking beyond us or in another direction. Perhaps they are

> " Children who have strong oral-language skills often have strong reading and writing skills. In contrast, children with oral-language problems are at higher risk of reading and writing difficulties (Scarborough, 2001). "

Photo: Alison Billman

looking at us, but their eyes are glazed over. Perhaps they aren't responding to what we are saying—no comments, no head nods, no "mm-hmm"s or "really"s. This can be discouraging, especially for young children trying so desperately to be understood.

We need to send young children signals that we are listening to them. If you are too busy or distracted to do that, let them know: "Just a minute—I really want to hear what you are saying." Hold your finger up until you are ready to listen or suggest the child return in a few minutes (and if the child does not return, go find him or her).

Respond to Children and Expand on What They Say

The extent to which a mother responds to her child is one of the best predictors of many aspects of that child's language development (Bornstein, 1989; Landry, Smith, Miller-Loncar, &

Snack and mealtime are excellent times to converse with children. At one center we know, an adult is stationed at each table during lunch to facilitate conversation for all children.

Swank, 1997; Tamis-LeMonda, Bornstein, & Baumwell, 2001). Responsiveness to children undoubtedly also matters in child-care settings (Girolametto & Weitzman, 2002; Howes & Hamilton, 1992). Whenever possible, when a child says something to you, respond. Even if the child just grunts or points, respond to his or her attempt to communicate. For example:

CHILD: [*Points at a light on the ceiling.*]

TEACHER: You like the light.

CHILD: [*Grunts and gestures toward counter.*]

TEACHER: You'd want something from here? These crackers? [*Holds up crackers.*] This milk? [*Holds up milk.*]

> 66 *...when a child says something to you, respond. Even if the child just grunts or points, respond to his or her attempt to communicate.* 99

After you respond, if the situation warrants it, expand on the child's talk. In other words, take what a child says and put it into a larger language context. For example:

CHILD: [*Holds up a ball.*] Ball!

TEACHER: You found a ball.

CHILD: Apple.

TEACHER: Would you like an apple?

CHILD: [*Points to a photo of a dog on a book cover.*] Doggie!

TEACHER: What a cute doggie!

CHILD: Brown.

TEACHER: Yes, that's a brown dog.

Expanding on children's articulations, which is also known as "recasting," is one way to model more sophisticated language, as well as to recognize the importance of what children have to say.

Talk About Your Activities

Talk with children about what you are doing; it will expose them to language in general and to vocabulary for important aspects of their everyday lives. This is especially important for infants, since they will not use language to initiate conversation. "We need to change your diaper. Oh, that diaper is stinky! We need to put it in the diaper pail." It is amazing how much children will learn from this!

Get Beyond the Here and Now

Some child-care providers devote most of their talk to commands ("Sit down," "Careful," "Walk") and management ("Time for lunch," "Naptime," "Over there"). Mothers who talk beyond the here and now—who talk about events of yesterday or tomorrow, describe or explain things, tell stories, and so on—raise children with stronger language and literacy skills (DeTemple, 2001; Dickinson, 2001a; McCartney, 1984). We believe the same is true for child-care providers.

Engage in Pretend Talk

Pretend talk involves talking about the nonliteral environment— or the environment that springs from one's imagination or past experiences. One study (Katz, 2001) showed that children whose mothers engaged in more pretend talk with them had stronger language skills later on. Here's an example of high-quality pretend talk between a mother and her 4-year-old child who are building with blocks:

> *Expanding on children's articulations . . . is one way to model more sophisticated language, as well as to recognize the importance of what children have to say.*

CHILD: Where am I going to put the chimney?

MOTHER: The chimney?

CHILD: Yup.

MOTHER: Why does it have to have a chimney?

CHILD: Yeah, a chimney. Where smoke comes out and Santa comes in.

MOTHER: Oh, yeah!

[*Dialogue continues.*]

(Katz, p. 65)

Here is an example between a mother and her 4-year-old child who are playing cars:

CHILD: You better watch out from that guy.

MOTHER: I know, he's gonna pass him.
Oh, he's gonna pass on the side.
[*Makes engine sounds.*] Whoops,
now he's gonna make a U-turn.
[*Makes more engine sounds.*]
Whoops, now he has to go slow.
He's in back of a bus.
[*Makes more engine sounds.*]

CHILD: How did he come back over that side?

MOTHER: I don't know; he's just driving around.
He likes to drive.

CHILD: You—he has to drive. He's the teacher,
right? He's the . . .
[*Dialogue continues.*]

(Katz, p. 66)

Pretend talk is a sophisticated kind of talk because it focuses on imagined, nonimmediate, and/or past experiences. In this sense it has many parallels to written language and therefore lays important groundwork for literacy later on.

Strong teachers seize many opportunities every day to talk with children. They also give many signals that they are listening carefully, as this teacher is.

Ask Open-Ended Questions

When you ask questions that can be answered with a single word, such as "yes," "no," or the name of an object or person, you are likely to get a one-word answer. When you ask open-ended questions, you are more likely to get more-complex answers— and the children answering are more likely to get practice in complex oral language. For example, if a child shows you a picture he or she has drawn, instead of asking "What is that?" try asking "Can you tell me about that?" See page 79 for more examples of open-ended questions.

Tell Stories

Research suggests that children exposed to more narratives develop stronger language and literacy skills (Beals, 2001). So tell everyday stories about things that have happened or will happen to you, to a child in the class, or to the whole group. We all know that children love to hear stories about funny things they have said, about things the group has done together, or about embarrassing things that have happened to us. For example, Nell has a story about accidentally sitting on a plate of freshly frosted cookies. Children love that one! We even teach children to use conversational prompts to encourage storytelling at home, such as "Tell me a story," "What happened next?" and "When were you embarrassed?"

Tell and *Explain*

Explanatory talk is another hallmark of a quality oral-language environment (Beals & Snow, 1994; Hart & Risley, 1995). Don't just tell children to do something; explain why they should do it. (For example, "Hang on with two hands. You might spill.") Don't just tell children not to do something, explain why they shouldn't do it and state it positively so that they know what to do. (For example, "Walk in the hallway. I'm concerned you'll fall." Instead of "Don't run.") Explain how things work, why you do things, what led to particular decisions, and so on.

Take Advantage of Quiet Times for Talk

As a child-care provider, Susan always enjoyed changing children's diapers. Why? Because it assured her some quiet, one-on-one time with every child every day. Diaper-changing time, mealtime, settling in for nap time—these are wonderful times to converse with individual children. (See chapter 11 for more information on taking advantage of moments like these.) And they may be the best times—research suggests that having lengthy conversations with one child during group time may not be advantageous to all the children's language development (Dickinson, 2001a). Restrict lengthy one-to-one conversations to one-on-one time or, at most, small-group time.

Sing, Sing a Song

In chapter 5, we stress that singing songs can promote phonological awareness development. We believe it can also help develop other aspects of language, such as vocabulary (words) and syntax (the way words are strung together). By singing along with you or singing songs on their own, children give their memories a good workout as they try to remember the words of the song. And, of course, enjoying music together is an important part of the human experience in its own right. See the chart to the left for a list of songs posted in one teacher's classroom.

♫ Songs We Know ♫

Itsy Bitsy Spider
Five Little Ducks
Wheels on the Bus
Ten in the Bed
Miss Mary Mack
Apples and Bananas
Turn - Around
Did You Feed My Cow?
Mama's Little Baby Loves...
What Is Your Name?
This Is the Way We Get Up
Put Your Hands in the Air

An illustrated list of songs the class knows can be a source of pride and a good resource for children and teachers alike.

Use a Rich, but Not Too Rich, Vocabulary

Researchers have suggested applying "the Goldilocks principle" to our vocabulary use. That is, when we interact with children, we should not use too many new words or too few new words—but just the right number of new words. Of course, you're now wondering, what is the right number of new words? There is no magic formula. We have to read children continually to figure out the right number. Are they confused or overwhelmed, or are they keeping up with you?

Use Vocabulary in Supportive Contexts

How you use new words can determine whether children make those words their own (for example, Tabors, Beals, & Weizman, 2001). Here are some guidelines for choosing and using words that are unfamiliar to children:

Use Words That Really Fit

Don't use a word that is not quite right for the sake of teaching a new word. This will only confuse or mislead children. Conversely, if a particular word is perfect for a situation, don't be afraid to use it. We remember hearing a story of a toddler who came to her center with a small bag of jelly beans. Her teacher asked, "What are those?" expecting the child to say "Jelly beans" or "Candy." The child replied, "A choking hazard!" Clearly, this child's parents weren't afraid to call a choking hazard a choking hazard—and the child learned the term!

Provide Language-Based and Visual Clues for Figuring Out New Words

Make sure the words you say around a new word give clues to the new word's meaning. For example, instead of saying "That's a llama," say "That's an animal called a llama. It's sort of like a camel." Instead of saying "She's vain," say "She thinks about her good looks all day long—she's vain."

Whenever possible, provide children not only with language-based clues to word meaning, but with visual clues as well. For example, point to a photograph or a picture that depicts the word, hold up the actual object you are naming, act out the word in facial expression or gesture, and so on.

Include Taxonomic Information

An interest in taxonomy—the classification of plants, animals, and objects into categories—seems to be one of the things that separates societies with formal schooling from societies where few or no people go to school (Cole, 1990; Rogoff & Chavajay, 1995). When defining words for children, include taxonomic information. Knowing that a donkey is a type of animal, that the Fourth of July is a holiday, and that a rhombus is a shape, for example, helps children understand how the word fits into a larger context. Of course, you shouldn't stop there. Provide synonyms, descriptions, and examples too.

Promote Curiosity About Words

We want to develop children who are curious about words— who notice when they hear a word they don't know, who ask about the meaning of words, who let you know when they don't understand. Some researchers have referred to this as

In describing familiar objects, encourage children to discuss the categories into which those objects fall. For example, a doll is a kind of toy and a shirt is a type of clothing.

"word consciousness" (Graves & Watts-Taffe, 2002). To help develop word consciousness

✳ **praise children when they ask about a word they don't know.** You might say

- "Good question!"

- "I'm glad you asked about that."

- "That's great you asked about a word you don't know."

✳ **praise children when they let you know they don't understand.** You might say

- "Thanks for letting me know you don't understand."

- "Great job thinking about what I'm saying."

- "Good" (and go on to explain what they didn't understand).

✳ **model questions and curiosity about words.** You might say

- "What does that mean?" Ask this question on those rare occasions when a child uses a word, perhaps from a television program he or she has watched, that you don't know. Also, ask that question about words that children make up. For example, Susan's son used the word *frinkle* in a sentence. Turns out he had made up a word to describe "fat wrinkles"!

- "I wonder if that's called _____ because of _____."

- "Isn't that a wonderful word?!"

- "Let me tell you about a word I just learned."

✳ **generate interest in words.** You might

- read books with interesting words or word play. (See book lists in chapters 4 and 5.)

- use and introduce words with interesting sounds and/or meanings, such as *squishy*, *platypus*, and *verbose*.

Be on the Lookout for Oral-Language Problems

As noted at the outset of this chapter, children who have difficulties with oral language are at a greater risk for later difficulties with written language (Scarborough, 2001). It is beyond the scope of this book to talk in depth about "normal" language development or signs of language problems. If your knowledge in this area is weak, build it up by spending time at Web sites of organizations such as the National Association for the Education of Young Children (www.naeyc.org) and the American Speech–Language–Hearing Association (www.asha.org). If you see signs of a significant language delay or problem in a child, obtain his or her parents' permission to contact a speech and language specialist for a consultation—or encourage the parents themselves to contact a specialist. Some states, such as Michigan, even provide free language testing and, if needed, intervention for young children. Making sure children get the help they need now could make a big difference to their literacy development later.

Photo: Raymond Coutu

Children's oral language can be enhanced with the use of props and involvement by adults.

If you choose to teach baby signs, use oral language along with them. Once children can say the words, encourage them to speak as well as sign until they don't need to sign any longer. (Of course, if a child is being raised to use American Sign Language, Total Communication, or another system, encourage him or her to continue using it, because, unlike baby signs, that is his or her primary and, perhaps, permanent form of interpersonal communication.)

Provide Props That Promote Oral Language

Include microphones, old telephones, puppets, flannel boards, even paper-towel tubes. These and other props can encourage oral-language interaction. So try to make them available, model their use, and encourage children to use them in their play.

Make Time for Extended Discourse

Finally, a major difference between effective and less effective oral-language environments is the amount of extended discourse that occurs (Dickinson, 2001b). Extended discourse is a back-and-forth exchange on a single topic, made up of questions and comments that build off of one another. Limited discourse, on the other hand, is made up of a single question or comment followed by a single response. Extended discourse promotes not only sophisticated language development but also cognitive development, because talking at length about a single topic helps children look at it from many angles, integrate information across sources, make connections, and so on.

Implementing all of the strategies on pages 46–59 at once will probably be overwhelming. So select a couple and add others as those become comfortable. Your effort will be well worth it!

Helping Families Develop Children's Oral Language

As research cited throughout this chapter indicates, how families talk with their children is one of the most important factors in children's oral-language and later literacy development. Yet few parenting classes, books, or TV shows address this. As such, many families know little about supporting oral-language development. You can help fill this gap by

* sending home handouts periodically with suggestions (like those in this chapter) for promoting oral language.

* modeling good oral-language interaction when families are observing you with their children.

* holding occasional parent workshops on how oral language develops and how to support it. Project EASE is a good example of a series of parent workshops that has been shown to make measurable differences in children's language development (Jordan, Snow, & Porche, 2000). Coaches held one workshop per month for five months, each on a different theme related to language interaction:

  • words, words, words (learning and using new vocabulary)

  • telling personal-event narratives (telling stories of things that have happened to you)

  • discussing storybook narratives (talking about stories in books)

  • discussing information-rich books

  • learning about letters and sounds

At the workshops coaches explained that month's theme and gave suggestions and examples of effective interaction, such as how to explain a new word to a child (see discussion earlier in this chapter), related to the theme. Workshops were immediately followed by a parent-child practice activity, and parents were given a take-home guide related to the theme. For the three weeks following the workshop, coaches provided parents with scripted activities on the theme (for example, discussions to have around specific children's story books). Even this relatively small intervention led to real changes in kindergarten children's vocabulary, story comprehension, and story sequencing.

Things *Not* to Do When Talking With Children

Just as there are things you can do to promote oral-language development, there are things you can do that may hinder oral-language development. Here are a few:

Correcting Children

It is widely believed that correcting young children's grammar or pronunciation is not a good idea (Cazden, 1969) because it can discourage children and is often not effective in turning the situation around. So instead of correcting what children say, recast it. For example:

CHILD: I goed to the potty.

TEACHER: You went to the potty. Good.

—

CHILD: I want pasketti.

TEACHER: Okay, you can have some spaghetti.

When you recast, be sure to speak naturally. Do not overemphasize the word that the child misspoke. If a child mistakes a word's meaning, again, don't correct. Instead, say something like "Oh, we usually use the word _____ for that" or "_____ means more like _____."

Demanding "Complete Sentences"

Most Harvard graduates often don't speak in complete sentences—so why should we expect preschoolers to? "Sentence" is a written-language concept and not an oral-language concept. When someone says, "How are you doing?" it is just fine to say, "Fine," rather than, "I am doing fine." Give children the same option. Of course, if a child doesn't use enough words for you to understand his or her message, then it is appropriate to ask for clarification or give your interpretation for the child to reject or confirm.

Dismissing Children's Home Language

The ability to speak more than one language or in more than one dialect is an asset, not a deficit, because it allows a person to communicate in multiple settings. Evidence even suggests

> *Evidence…suggests that children who speak more than one language become more developmentally advanced in their abilities to think and talk about their language (metalinguistic awareness) than children who speak only one language* (Bialystok, 2001).

that children who speak more than one language become more developmentally advanced in their abilities to think and talk about language (metalinguistic awareness) than children who speak only one language (Bialystok, 2001). So rather than dismissing children's home language, encourage them to use it, teach it to you and others, and value it. For example, in Susan's program, one child taught all the children how to sing "Happy Birthday" in Korean. Now on birthdays, children sing "Happy Birthday" in both languages.

Insisting on a "Quiet" Room During Learning Times

Make sure children are seen and heard. Nell recalls a time when she was doing cooperative learning with children. The children were talking with one another in small groups about the work they were doing: sorting and classifying leaves. The classroom was buzzing with conversation. Nell was pleased . . . until an administrator came by and asked what was going on. She explained what the children were doing and the value of such activity. The administrator responded, "It's fine if they do cooperative learning, as long as they don't talk"! The notion that a quiet classroom is an ideal classroom is still out there, but it contrasts sharply with what we know about the importance of talk in a classroom. While it is important for children to know when and how to use their "inside voices," children need to be able to talk to one another, and to you, if their oral language is to develop.

Concluding Thoughts

We are dedicated teachers and researchers of literacy education, committed to building children's knowledge of print. Yet when we enter an early childhood environment, we are as concerned about the kind of talk going on as we are about the kind of print on the walls or reading activities in the schedule. Oral-language development is important to literacy development and in its own right. We hope this chapter has given you some tools for building it in children.

Give a Little Listen!

In the hustle and bustle of the day, it is hard to stop and reflect on what we are saying to children and what children are saying to us. A great way to address this is to tape-record yourself interacting with children and then listen to the recording later. Small portable tape recorders can be purchased at most discount stores for as little as $10. Some models are small enough to hook to your belt so they'll move with you. Of course, chances are, the more you spend on the tape recorder, the higher the sound quality will be. Some teachers prefer being videotaped so they can observe their nonverbal communication with children as well.

Think about the strategies for promoting oral-language development, and ways to hinder it (i.e., the "don't"s), from this chapter and listen for evidence of them in the recording. Also keep an ear out for patterns such as which children you speak with too often or too infrequently; whether most of what you say is positive, negative, or neutral; and so on. You may also want to invite a colleague to listen to or view tapes with you; he or she might notice things you might not notice.

The wordless picture book Creepy Castle (Goodall, 1975) was used in research on knowledge of storybook language among children who were read to frequently (Purcell-Gates, 1988).

developed sophisticated knowledge of written language and how it differs from oral language. Later research showed that children who have not been read to by parents enough to develop this knowledge got it from being read to by teachers (Purcell-Gates, McIntyre, & Freppon, 1995). So even if the parents of children in your care are not reading to them at home—especially if parents are not reading to them at home—you can make an important difference in their literacy development by doing that while they're with you.

In this chapter, we describe how you can use Read Aloud to support five important aspects of literacy development:

- letter-sound knowledge
- concepts of print
- vocabulary
- comprehension
- world knowledge

Read Aloud can support other areas of development as well, such as phonological awareness (see chapter 5) and even gross motor development (see chapter 10). But by focusing on letter-sound knowledge, concepts of print, vocabulary, comprehension, and world knowledge, we give you plenty of ideas for making the most of Read Aloud.

The When, Where, What, Why, Who, and How of Read Aloud

When?

Given the many benefits of Read Aloud, we believe that teachers should read to infants, toddlers, and preschoolers every day, especially when they are in their best state for learning, meaning not tired, wild, or fussy.

Where?

Read Aloud can happen almost anywhere. In fact, in chapter 10 we talk about the value of reading aloud outdoors! Make sure children are comfortable and close enough to hear your voice and see the book's pictures. If children have difficulty sitting together without bothering one another, have each child sit on a carpet square or spot on the rug marked with his or her name or a symbol of some sort.

What?

There are countless wonderful books to read aloud to young children. We have listed some in this chapter on page 89 and throughout this book, but there are many more where those came from! See chapter 7 for information about selecting books wisely and obtaining them inexpensively. The bottom line is to be sure that the books, not to mention other materials such as excerpts from children's magazines, signs, or posters, that you read aloud are worth the time spent reading them—that they are developmentally appropriate, interesting or enjoyable, and of real quality. Many books for children—especially those sold at supermarkets or dollar stores or those based on TV or movie characters—are poorly written and do not expose children to quality writing.

Why?

Read Aloud builds so many literacy skills, including the ones at the heart of this chapter: letter-sound knowledge, concepts of print, vocabulary, comprehension, and world knowledge. It can also be a great source of enjoyment for young children. Take a moment to look at the photos in this chapter. Children are captivated and happy. And Read Aloud (especially lap reading which we describe later) provides bonding time for you and children.

Who?

As the teacher, you should be the primary person who reads aloud, but there are other options too. As discussed in chapter 9, children may enjoy listening to books at a listening center or watching books on video. (See box entitled "Videos and DVDs for Read Aloud" on page 68.) Children may also enjoy guest readers such as family members, other teachers, or a police officer, doctor, or other member of the community. Most adults are happy to share a favorite book with a group of young children, which sends an important message about the value of literacy.

Have Children Make Their Own Alphabet Books

A wonderful way for children to develop their understanding of alphabet books and to strengthen their alphabet knowledge is to make their own alphabet books (with lots of help from you, of course). You can make a class alphabet book by having each child create a page or two. Better yet, you can have each child make his or her own individual book. (This takes some time but is well worth it, and it's a great way to involve volunteers.) Start by having children select snapshots, clip magazine photos, and create drawings of people and things that are important to them, such as a favorite toy, family member, and food. Then have them paste the snapshots, photos, and drawings onto pages based on their first letter. You might write a letter, upper- and lowercase, on each page in advance, or you might have children write the letters themselves. Older children can help you assemble the book by singing the alphabet song slowly and placing the pages in that order. Books can be laminated and bound with string, metal fasteners, or binding from a local copy shop.

Read the books aloud at the children's request, and encourage families to do the same by sending the books home with written or oral instructions, such as those listed to the left.

Treat Alphabet Books As More Than Just Vehicles for Alphabet Learning

You can use alphabet books for much more than letter-sound instruction. Some books have engaging stories, some have photographs or illustrations worth pouring over, some contain important and interesting information. (See box entitled "Fourteen Fabulous Alphabet Books" on pages 71–72.) It would be a shame—and, let's face it, a bore—to overlook all of that and just focus on letters and sounds. As a rule of thumb, attend to two or three aspects of the book, such as the story, the illustrations, and the alphabet, when reading it. Or read it multiple times over a few days, concentrating on one aspect each time. That way, children get a lot of different things out of the book.

Here is the cover and a page from a child's self-made alphabet book.

Fourteen Fabulous Alphabet Books Book List

Alphabet books come in all kinds of shapes, sizes, and types. Some tell stories; some convey information. Some are simple, containing only a single word for each letter; some are complex, devoting whole paragraphs to each letter. Reading a variety of alphabet books over time holds children's interest... and yours.

A Is for Artist: A Getty Museum Alphabet
J. Paul Getty Museum, 1997
In this book, a classic work of art is paired with each letter of the alphabet, with an object in the work beginning with that letter. After you read the name of the object, toddlers may enjoy pointing it out in the work. Preschoolers

may enjoy determining the object themselves by reading the word and/or examining the illustrations.

Alphabet City
by Stephen Johnson. Puffin, 1995
Johnson embeds alphabet letters in realistic illustrations of city scenes. Children will have great fun finding and calling out the

letters. For more information about this book, see page 189.

Alphabet Under Construction
by Denise Fleming. Henry Holt and Company, 2002
Denise Fleming's colorful, playful, and just plain wonderful illustrations make this book ultraengaging for toddlers and preschoolers.

Vowels often sound different when followed by /m/, /n/, and /r/.

Nasalization and r-control are also important concepts related to the English language. When a vowel sound is followed by a nasal sound (/m/ or /n/), the vowel often sounds different than when followed by other consonants. For example, say the words *ant* and *apple* to yourself. Listen to the first sound in each word. For many people, it sounds very different (though not as different for us, with our Midwestern accents).

Similarly, vowel sounds change when followed by an *r*. For example, the sound at the beginning of *art* or *orange* does not sound the same as at the beginning of *apple* or *ape*, *octopus* or *ogre*. When a nasalized or r-controlled word comes up in an alphabet book, children may become confused. They may not be able to hear that *art* starts with *a* or *orange* starts with *o*. Again, we are honest and explicit in these instances: "You can't hear /ă/ in *art*, but it starts with an *a*." Be sure not to distort words to try to make them sound like their spellings. Don't force an /ă/ in art, because it does not contain one. Doing so may confuse children, mislead them, and undermine their confidence in their ability to hear or pronounce.

Letter names can be confusing.

Unfortunately, the way we name English letters can create confusion. For example, many children think that *y* stands for /w/. Why? Because the name of the letter *y* begins with a /w/! And some children write the letter *w* with a *d*. Why? Because the name of the letter *w* begins with a /d/! Confused? So are young children. In fact, some scholars have even recommended we stop calling letters by their names and start calling them by their sounds. (McGuinness, 1997). We would not go that far because children encounter and need to know letter names in so many contexts, but we do want to be sensitive to potential confusion. For example, many books, puzzles, and other materials for young children use *elephant* to represent the letter *e*. However, the letter name for *l* (which actually begins with /e/) is heard at the beginning of *elephant*. We need to be explicit by telling children something like, "The very first sound in *elephant* is /e/; *e* stands for /e/." (For more information related to this, see chapter 5.)

When children express confusion or ask questions about letters and sounds, think carefully about what may be puzzling them. To learn more about sounds and letters in English, consult *Phonics for the Teacher of Reading* (Fox & Hull, 2002). If you are fascinated by the history of English spelling, you might enjoy *The American Way of Spelling: The Structure and Origins of American English Orthography* (Venezky, 1999).

Concepts of Print

Concepts of print are understandings about how texts work and how readers read, such as the correct way to open and hold a book, the fact that we read from left to right and top to bottom, and so on. How do we teach concepts of print through Read Aloud?

Hold, Open, and Read the Book in Front of Children

When we do this, we demonstrate the proper way to handle and navigate a book.

Point to Words As We Read

When we do this, we teach that we read words (not pictures); that we read words from left to right, top to bottom; and that spaces separate words. Big Books are enlarged versions of books, often three or four feet across and two feet tall. They are great not only for teaching concepts of print, but also for getting children to notice details in books such as punctuation marks and illustration techniques.

Talk About Parts of the Book

When we do this, we teach key vocabulary related to books, such as *front*, *back*, *first*, *last*, *beginning*, *ending*, *cover*, *title*, *author*, *illustrator*, *words*, *pictures*, and *letters*. Once children begin formal schooling, teachers sometimes mistakenly assume that children know these terms, so working on them now is a good idea.

Photo: Kelly Rae Chapin

Big books work especially well for teaching concepts of print. Here a teacher points to the picture, asking children, "Is this the part I read?"

Show How to Find a Particular Section of the Book

When we do this, we teach about features for navigating books—table of contents, index, heading, page numbers, and so on. Tell children that authors include these features to help readers find information. Then use the features to look up information in response to a child's question, such as "How are alligators and crocodiles different?" Children who are used to seeing books read in their entirety from beginning to end may be surprised to see you read just a portion of the book that you look up using navigational features. Explain that people read in different ways depending on the type of book and their purpose for reading.

You don't have to use only books to teach concepts of print. Many concepts, such as reading from left to right, can be taught using recipes, poems, magazine articles, and many other kinds of text. Furthermore, children will learn best not just by watching you, but also by trying things out themselves. An infant or toddler could sit on your lap and help you turn pages. A preschooler could help you find the cover, title, and author of a book. That said, do not spend a lot of time on concepts of print. If you expose children to literacy on a regular basis, especially with book reading, most of them will pick up many concepts on their own (Clay, 1993). Observing what children have and have not learned and then teaching responsively should be sufficient.

Vocabulary

When we take time to explain and talk about important new words during Read Aloud, it can make a big difference in children's vocabulary development (Beck, McKeown, & Kucan, 2003; Whitehurst, Arnold, et al., 1994; Whitehurst, Epstein, et al., 1994). In this section we describe Text Talk, a technique for developing children's vocabulary during Read Aloud (Beck & McKeown, 2001). Whether you use this approach, other approaches (for example, dialogic reading, Zevenbergen & Whitehurst, 2003), or your own approach, a focus on vocabulary during Read Aloud is likely to benefit your children.

Text Talk

Text Talk, developed by Isabel Beck and Margaret McKeown, is an approach to Read Aloud designed to promote vocabulary and reading comprehension (Beck & McKeown, 2001; McKeown & Beck, 2003). The approach has been shown to have benefits for kindergartners and first graders, and we believe it has benefits for somewhat younger children as well, provided that the texts, words, and comprehension foci selected are appropriate to their age.

Text Talk involves a strong focus on vocabulary and comprehension before, during, and after Read Aloud.

Before Read Aloud

If you are using lesson plans for Text Talk developed by others, such as those available in a book (for example, Beck & McKeown, 2001), online (http://www.readwritethink.org/lessons/lesson_view.asp?id=25), or in a commercial program (for example, Scholastic's Text Talk program), follow their recommendations for choosing target vocabulary and comprehension goals. If you are developing your own Text Talk lesson plans, preview the book to be read aloud looking for vocabulary that may be unfamiliar to children. If you were going to read *Corduroy* (Freeman, 1968), you might choose *sighed* and *enormous*. You should also consider the book in terms of comprehension—what do you want to make sure children understand?

During Read Aloud

Provide brief explanations of words likely to be unfamiliar to children. These explanations need to be brief and understandable to young children, so don't necessarily provide formal dictionary definitions. For example:

> "When people are *amusing*, they are usually funny or they make you happy to watch them. A clown at a circus is amusing."

> "When someone is a *nuisance*, he or she is bothering you."

> (Beck et al., 2002, p. 55)

More elaborate explanations and word work are provided after reading.

66 *When we take time to explain and talk about important new words during Read Aloud, it can make a big difference in children's vocabulary development* (Beck et al., 2003; Whitehurst et al., 1994). 99

The Importance of Repeated Reading

What is one thing that many children who read early and well have in common? They have heard books read aloud to them over and over again (Durkin, 1966). We believe that hearing the same books repeatedly allows children to internalize their features, such as their rhyme and story structure. It also allows them to focus on things they wouldn't during a first reading, such as the print rather than just the pictures or the meaning of a particular word. Allow children to suggest favorite books they want to hear again . . . and again . . . and again. Even if you feel you just can't read that book one more time, do, knowing that it is important for children's literacy development.

For comprehension development, ask open-ended questions—not just questions for which there is a "known" answer or that can be answered with a simple yes or no. (See the chart on page 79 for ideas.) Follow up on children's responses by doing things such as rereading a relevant portion of the book or explaining the child's comment in a way that might be more understandable to the other children.

Show the book's illustrations to children, but not until after the text on the page has been read and discussed. This will focus children on processing the language of the text.

After Read Aloud

Focus on vocabulary development with activities like these:

- revisiting the portion of the book where the target word was used

- having children repeat the word

- providing a brief explanation of the word

- asking for children's further thoughts on the target word's meaning

- using the target word in some example sentences and then having children do the same thing

- seeing how the target word can be used in different contexts to provide a more complete understanding of what the word means

- having children say the word once again to reinforce it in their minds

For example, imagine that a teacher reads aloud a book that includes the word *absurd*. After she has reviewed the word *absurd* as it appeared in the book, she has the children repeat the word and then provides a brief explanation of what the word means. After this, the teacher provides an example in context (different from the book's), such as "If I told you that your teacher was going to stand on his/her head to teach you—that would be absurd. If someone told you that dogs could fly—that would be absurd" (McKeown & Beck, 2003, p. 165). The children can also be asked to make decisions about whether something is absurd

Comparison of Closed and Open Questions and Answers

Baseline Classroom

Questions	Responses
Is he a new toy or an old toy?	Old.
Who is Joe? He's the what?	Baby.
Think back in the story. They went to pick up his…	Big sister.
Do you think Nelle is going to be happy or mad?	Mad.
Somebody else had already what?	Found him.
Was she being nice to her little brother?	Yeah.

Text Talk Classroom

Questions	Responses
How did the other kids like Stephanie's ponytail?	First they liked it when she didn't have it to her ear, and then they kept calling her ugly, and now they're gonna be jealous, real jealous.
What's going on?	George got into trouble anyway.
What's the problem with having a fawn as a pet?	Cause he'll eat everything. He's like a goat.
Charlie looked at the girls and purred. What's that tell us?	The girls are happy that they might have found him.
Why would termites be a worry for the owl?	Because the termites might eat the owl's home cause it's made out of wood.
What happened?	The people saw the signmaker and chased him into the woods and they thought that the signmaker did it, but the boy did.

(McKeown & Beck, 2003, p. 164)

> *Allow children to suggest favorite books they want to hear again . . . and again . . . and again. Even if you feel you just can't read that book one more time, do, knowing that it is important for children's literacy development.*

or makes sense, such as in the following examples: "I have a singing cow for a pet." [absurd] or "Last night I watched a movie on TV." [makes sense] (McKeown & Beck, 2003, p. 165). Last, children have the opportunity to give their own examples of something absurd. These examples can be quite memorable—in one case a child's example for the word *reluctant* was "I would be reluctant to change a baby's diaper!"

Summary

Look for opportunities to use target words in conversations. And encourage children to use them in conversations, too. Some children enjoy impressing their parents with newly acquired terms.

Consider these four sentences from *Come Along, Daisy!* (Simmons, 1997):

> Something big stirred underneath her. Daisy shivered. She scrambled up onto the riverbank. Then something screeched in the sky above!

In these sentences alone several words—wonderful words— are likely to be new to children. Children's books are a terrific source of new words. Paying attention to these words is important to children's literacy development.

Comprehension

In our opinion, comprehension, or the ability to make meaning from text, is the most important part of reading and, therefore, should be emphasized in your teaching. With every Read Aloud we can help children construct meaning of the text being read and develop knowledge, skills, and habits that help them understand other texts. For instance, when we ask children what is going to happen next in a story, we suggest that good readers make predictions as they read. When we talk with children about the important ideas in an information book, we help them focus on main ideas. When we ask children to make connections between their own lives and a book, we teach them one of the most important habits of a good reader. In this section we discuss three effective ways to build comprehension skills through Read Aloud: interactive reading, sustained conversation, and deliberate teaching.

Interactive Reading

Most scholars (see, for example, van Kleeck, Stahl, & Bauer, 2003) suggest making Read Aloud interactive to build comprehension. In other words, we usually shouldn't read a book straight through without stopping. We shouldn't have children sit passively, listening to us read. Rather, we should give children opportunities to point, make comments, ask questions, and engage in conversations related to the book. And we should make comments and ask questions related to the book as well.

We need to make sure that our comments and questions are varied and that many focus on higher-order thinking. In other words, we should not ask only questions with simple right or wrong answers that can be found easily in the text. Questions that start with "Why do you think . . ." "Have you ever . . ." and the like can promote the kind of thinking associated with deep comprehension. In the chart on page 83 we present many different kinds of comments and questions you can use in Read Aloud.

A Sustained Conversation About *Goldilocks and the Three Bears*, Led by Researcher Lesley Mandel Morrow

I recently led a discussion with four-year-olds after reading *Goldilocks and the Three Bears*. I asked who were the good and the bad characters. Hands waved in the air and Jennifer answered, "Goldilocks was good and the bears were bad." When I asked Jennifer why she thought that, she said, "Well, the bears scared Goldilocks."

Another hand went up and Tim said, "No, that's not right. The bears are good and Goldilocks is bad. Goldilocks went into the bears' house when they weren't home. She ate their food and didn't even ask."

"That's right," said Megan, "and she broke their chair and went to sleep in their bed and didn't even ask if it was okay."

Chris chimed in, "Yeah, Goldilocks was really bad. She did a lot of bad things because she didn't ask if she could."

"Would you go into a stranger's house and do the things Goldilocks did?" I asked. The whole group called out in unison "Nooooo." I asked why not. Sara answered, "Because that is bad. It's like stealing. She was naughty. If the cops found out, I bet they will arrest her."

(Morrow, 1989, p. 92)

Sustained Conversation

When making comments and asking questions, don't rely on the I–R–E pattern, in which the teacher Initiates a question, the child Responds, the teacher Evaluates the response, with the teacher repeating the pattern by initiating a new question that is unrelated to the first one (Cazden, 1988; Mehan, 1979; Sinclair & Coulthard, 1975). For example:

TEACHER: What's this? [*Points to part of an illustration in a storybook.*]

CHILD: A panda bear.

TEACHER: Right.

TEACHER: Who's that? [*Points to another part of the illustration in the storybook.*]

CHILD: Maisy.

TEACHER: Yes.

(and so on)

Research shows that in elementary, middle, and high school classrooms where the I–R–E pattern is used, students show less growth in comprehension than in classrooms where sustained conversations, with students taking turns speaking on the same topic and/or point, are encouraged (Nystrand, Gamoran, Kachur, & Pendergast, 1997; Saunders & Goldenberg, 1999). Research with preschoolers also suggests that sustained conversation between teacher and child is important—a real conversation about the book, with both parties trying to understand its meaning together (Dickinson & Smith, 1994). The box on page 81 contains an example of a sustained conversation about text.

Deliberate Teaching

If Read Aloud is one of the most important tools for developing literacy, it makes sense to be deliberate in our approach to it. That means we should select Read Aloud books carefully (see chapter 7) and, whenever possible, read through them ahead of time if they are unfamiliar to us. We should also set specific goals for children beyond engagement. To do that, select one or two areas as the primary focus of your Read Aloud. For ideas, see the

Some Types of Questions and Comments We Can Make During Read Aloud to Build Comprehension

Question/ Comment type	Examples	Especially good to use when...
Factual Detail	Where does this story take place? What is the name of a baby goat?	the detail is important to understanding the text.
Inferential	Why did the boy run back home? Why do mice avoid snakes?	the text does not ask the question directly, but the answer is important.
Opinion	What do you think they should do? What's your opinion on this?	there is a potential for many different answers.
Bridging to Experience	Have you ever had a fight with your brother? Have you . . .	text content may relate to child's experiences.
Predicting	What do you think will happen next? What will it tell about now?	emphasizing reading for purpose or using text structure.
Focusing on Text Structure	What is the problem for this boy? How are dogs and cats the same and different?	teaching story structure or an informational text structure such as compare/contrast.
Labeling	Do you know what that is called? What does . . . mean?	focusing on developing the child's vocabulary.
Intertextual Links	Does that remind you of another book we have read?	text or content is similar to something else you have read.
Writing Project Links	Is there anything there we can use in our writing? Let's remember . . .	text relates closely to a writing project.
Adopting Authorship	If you were the author, how would you end the story?	focusing on teaching children to think like authors.
Evaluative	Did you find that funny?	children are not evaluating text spontaneously.
Pointing Out	Look at that fox hidden there. Look at how the print is larger.	children are unlikely to notice an important detail on their own.
Explaining	These are what the water comes through. A buffet is . . .	dealing with an unfamiliar word, concept, plot, etc.
Summarizing	So what was this whole part of the book about?	teaching children to sum up, synthesize.

Other kinds of comprehension-building talk that might go on during Read Aloud

Type of talk	Explanation/Example	Especially good to use when...
Chiming In	Children read part of the text along with you.	text is very familiar or predictable.
Elaborating	Child makes a comment like "yuck" and you elaborate on it.	child needs to work on expanding his/her speech.
Feedback	Child makes comment, you affirm it: "Yes, I think so too."	encouraging children to comment on the text.
Managing	Let's go on to the next page now. Let's go back and read again.	children are not sure of what you are doing.

Do not attempt all of these different kinds of questions or comments in one reading, or to ask so many questions or make so many comments that it interrupts the flow of the reading. That may only make the reading hard to follow and frustrate children.   (Some categories from Neuman, 1996.)

first column in the chart on page 83 or the expectations discussed in chapter 1. Next, plan out some questions or comments you will make. Let's say you chose to focus on "Focusing on Text Structure" using the storybook *Swimmy* (Lionni, 1963); you may ask a number of questions and make a number of comments related to key story elements—characters, setting, problem, and resolution. If you chose to focus on intertextual links you might plan questions and comments comparing your chosen book for the day with another book by the same author or with similar characteristics that you read aloud earlier in the week. Be thoughtful and deliberate about the reading knowledge, skills, and habits that you are teaching in a Read Aloud.

Photo: Alison Billman

World Knowledge

What children know (and don't know) about the world around them—about people, places, and things—has an enormous impact on their literacy (Wilson & Anderson, 1986). How can students comprehend a science textbook if they don't know the things that the author assumes they know? How can they write about animal habitats if they know little about either animals or habitats? Moreover, how much children read (and are read to) seems to affect what they know, because reading is a powerful way to build world knowledge (Stanovich, 1986).

The chart on page 85 lists a few books you can use to build basic knowledge that we all want young children to have. Of course, there are many other wonderful titles out there—the possibilities are endless!

Building World Knowledge Through a Combination of Books and Real-Life Experiences

Research with elementary-aged children suggests that the combination of books or other texts and real-life or hands-on experiences is the most powerful for learning (Anderson & Guthrie, 1999; Palincsar & Magnusson, 2000). We think this is also true for younger children.

Books for Building World Knowledge

You can use	To build knowledge about
My First Word Board Book. Dorling Kindersley, 1997	words for all sorts of objects (infants, toddlers).
Baby Faces by Margaret Miller. Little Simon, 1998	feelings (infants, toddlers).
Fuzzy Yellow Ducklings by Matthew Van Fleet. Dial Books for Young Readers, 1995	shapes, colors, textures, animals (infants, toddlers).
A Rainbow All Around Me by Sandra L. Pinkney. Photographs by Myles C. Pinkney. Scholastic, 2002	colors, description (toddlers, preschoolers).
Who Uses This? by Margaret Miller. Scholastic, 1990	tools, professions (toddlers, preschoolers).
Piggies by Audrey Wood. Illustrated by Don Wood, 1997	opposites (toddlers, preschoolers).
About Birds: A Guide for Children by Cathryn Sill. Illustrated by John Sill. Peachtree, 1991	birds (preschoolers).
Hello Ocean by Pam Muñoz Ryan. Illustrated by Mark Astrella. Scholastic, 2001	senses (preschoolers).
My Car by Byron Barton. Greenwillow Books, 2001	cars, car parts (preschoolers).

You can create that combination using a method called Experience-Text-Relationship or E-T-R (Tharp, 1982). After you select a text for Read Aloud, keeping in mind the goal of building world knowledge, follow these three phases:

Experience (E) Ask children about experiences they have had related to the text. Questions beginning with "Have you ever . . ." or "Do you remember. . ." often work well. If possible, provide experiences related to the text, as in the examples on pages 86–88.

Text (T) Read aloud the text you chose, making sure children are making sense of it by asking questions and providing explanations at points where you think understanding may be breaking down.

Relationship (R) After reading, or, in some cases, as you read, draw children's attention to the ways their experiences relate to and diverge from those in the text by asking questions such as "How is that like what happened to you?" or making comments such as "That's a lot like what Maria saw when she went camping."

Bibliotherapy

This is a fancy word for the notion of using books to work through personal problems, which can be helpful to young children (Aiex, 2005). For example, books like *Night Shift Daddy* (Spinelli, 2000) or *When Mama Comes Home Tonight* (Spinelli, 1998) may help children deal with separation from their parents. A book like *It's Okay to Be Different* (Parr, 2001) may help children cope with and even take pride in differences in their background, skills, and interests. Of course, we need to be cautious when applying bibliotherapy since most of us are not trained therapists. That said, talking about issues during Read Aloud can bring comfort and perspective to children.

Example E-T-R for Infants Using *Peek-a-Boo!* by Roberta Grobel Intrater. This book features color photographs of babies and toddlers peeking at the camera with various expressions, props, and poses.

E: Play peek-a-boo with the infant(s). While playing, say "We are playing peek-a-boo."

T: Read *Peek-a-Boo!*, pronouncing the term *peek-a-boo* in the same way you did while playing peek-a-boo. Say, "The babies are playing peek-a-boo."

R: Explain "The babies are playing peek-a-boo. We play peek-a-boo." Play peek-a-boo with the infant using props and terms from the book, showing him or her pages that match your play.

Example E-T-R for Toddlers Using *Insects and Crawly Creatures* by Angela Royston, photographs by Jerry Young. This book contains photographs of and basic information about common insects such as ladybugs and flies.

E: Take children on a quest for insects. Around and under logs and rocks and on or near trees and plants are good places to look. Collect insects in a container with air holes.

T: Return to the classroom to read *Insects and Crawly Creatures*. Rather than reading the whole book, you might read only pages about insects you found or might have found.

R: Have children compare the insects they found with those in the book. For example, if they found a ladybug, have them look at the photograph of a ladybug in the book and talk about similarities and differences between them. Read or reread the information about ladybugs so children can find out food they eat, provide that food, and place it in the insects' container. (You might want to have an adult-level insect guide on hand for those uncommon or hard-to-identify insects.)

A child studies insects using many types of text as resources.

Example E-T-R for Preschoolers Using *Pop! A Book About Bubbles* by Kimberly Brubaker Bradley, photographs by Margaret Miller. This book provides a great deal of information about bubbles and activities children can do with bubbles.

E: Provide children with an opportunity to explore bubbles by giving them a hands-on activity such as lathering up dish detergent at the sensory table or blowing bubbles outdoors. Talk with children about the bubbles, encouraging them to point out things they notice and wonder about.

T: Read *Pop! A Book About Bubbles.* Since this book is too long to read in one sitting for most groups, read those parts that relate most closely to things children did, noticed, or wondered about during the "experience" phase.

Photo: Raymond Coutu

Children explore bubbles by watching how they are blown and how they float.

R: Ask children questions that relate their bubble play to the information in the book. "Did your bubbles do that?" "What happened when you tried that?" You may want to return to the "experience" phase to give children time to experience what they have learned from the book and make more connections.

These are just a few examples of how literacy activities can be used to build world knowledge. Being deliberate in your choices about content to teach, selecting engaging books, and providing related hands-on activities is a powerful formula for building your children's knowledge of the world.

Concluding Thoughts

Read Aloud is a critical tool for building literacy (Anderson, Hiebert, Scott, & Wilkinson, 1985). As you have seen throughout this chapter (and will continue to see in forthcoming chapters), it can be used to build alphabet knowledge, concepts of print, vocabulary, comprehension, and world knowledge. Read Aloud is also a source of great joy. Make it a special time for you and the children in your care.

Great Read Alouds

Eight Great Read Alouds for Infants

Baby Animal Kisses by B. Saltzberg. Red Wagon, 2001

Baby Food by M. Miller. Little Simon, 2000

Blue Hat, Green Hat by S. Boynton. Simon & Schuster, 1984

Mr. Brown Can Moo! Can You? Dr. Seuss's Book of Wonderful Noises by Dr. Seuss. Random House, 1970

Peek-a-Who? by N. Laden. Chronicle Books, 2000

Tomie's Little Mother Goose by T. DePaola. G. P. Putnam and Sons, 1985

The Very Busy Spider by E. Carle. Philomel Books, 1984

Where Is Baby's Belly Button? by K. Katz. Simon & Schuster, 2000

Eight Great Read Alouds for Toddlers

Are Lemons Blue? Dorling Kindersley, 2003

Come Along, Daisy! by J. Simmons. Scholastic, 1997

Five Little Monkeys Jumping on the Bed by E. Christelow. Scholastic, 1989

Freight Train by D. Crews. Greenwillow Books, 1978

Hippos Go Berserk! by S. Boynton. Simon & Schuster, 1977

Jamberry by B. Degen. HarperFestival, 1994

The Little Red Hen by B. Barton. HarperFestival, 1993

The Snowy Day by E. J. Keats. Penguin Putnam, 1962

Eight Great Read Alouds for Younger Preschoolers

Corduroy by D. Freeman. Puffin, 1968

Feast for 10 by C. Falwell. Clarion Books, 1993

If You Give a Pig a Pancake by L. Numeroff. Illustrated by F. Bond. HarperCollins, 1998

It's the Bear! by J. Alborough. Candlewick Press, 1994

The Monster at the End of This Book by J. Stone. Illustrated by M. Smollin. Western Publishing Company, 1971

No Peas for Nellie by C. L. Demarest. Simon & Schuster, 1988

Swimmy by L. Lionni. Scholastic, 1963

The Three Bears by P. Galdone. Clarion Books, 1972

Eight Great Read Alouds for Older Preschoolers

Actual Size by S. Jenkins. Houghton Mifflin, 2004

The Family Book by T. Parr. Little, Brown, 2003

Little Apple: A Book of Thanks by B. Weninger and A. Moller. North-South Books, 2001

Piggie Pie by M. Palatini. Illustrated by H. Fine. Clarion Books, 1995

The Seven Silly Eaters by M. A. Hoberman. Illustrated by M. Frazee. Voyager Books, 2000

Two Eyes, a Nose, and a Mouth by R. G. Intrater. Scholastic, 2000

What Do You Do With a Tail Like This? by S. Jenkins and R. Page. Houghton Mifflin, 2003

A Wing on a Flea: A Book About Shapes by E. Emberley. Little, Brown, 2001

See other lists throughout the book. Also, see chapter 7 for a discussion on selecting books for use with young children.

As mentioned in chapter 4, when referring to a sound or sounds, we put slash marks around the letter or letters representing the sound or sounds. For example, we would write the sound at the beginning of the word *boy* like this: /b/.

- Songs, Nursery Rhymes and Rhyming Poems, and Tongue Twisters
- Word Games
- Stretching Words

Carrying out these activities will benefit your children because they will help them learn eight of the most important phonological awareness skills:

1. Separating words into syllables or beats
2. Recognizing rhyming words
3. Generating rhyming words
4. Recognizing words that start or end with the same sound
5. Generating words that start or end with the same sound
6. Blending sounds into words
7. Segmenting words into sounds
8. Moving sounds around to create new words

Why Are Phonological Awareness Skills So Important?

The ability to . . .	Will eventually help children to . . .
separate words into syllables or beats	break down a word into parts to spell or decode/read it.
recognize and generate rhyming words	use known words to decode new words. For example, to use *catch* to help them decode *batch*.
recognize and generate words that start or end with the same sound	learn to associate particular sounds with particular letters.
blend words into sounds	"sound out" words. For example, after saying a sound for each letter in the word *nap*—/n/ /a/ /p/—putting those sounds together to say *nap*.
segment words into sounds	spell words. For example, to hear the four sounds in the word *clap* so they can spell it.
move sounds around to create new words	use known words to figure out new words. For example, to use *corn* to help them decode the word *pork*.

In What Order Do Phonological Awareness Skills Develop?

Research indicates that there is a typical order in which phonological awareness skills are acquired (Anthony, Lonigan, Driscoll, Phillips, & Burgess, 2002). That said, of course, every child's development does not follow that order exactly. Sometimes children master segmenting before blending, for example. Sometimes they don't completely master one skill before moving on to the next. With that in mind, in general, the typical order goes as follows:

1. Skills involving syllables or beats will generally be acquired before those involving rhymes, which will in turn be acquired before those involving individual phonemes or sounds.

2. Recognizing-skills often come before generating-skills. For example, children are likely to recognize words that rhyme before they can generate words that rhyme.

3. Skills involving the beginnings of words are generally acquired before those involving the endings of words, followed finally by the middle of words.

4. The ability to blend will generally come before the ability to segment.

5. The ability to move sounds around to create new words is often one of the last skills acquired.

When planning phonological awareness activities, keep this sequence in mind—but also keep in mind what you know about individual children. As always, as the teacher, you are in the best position to know which skills children have acquired, which they are working on, and which are too difficult for them.

Songs, Nursery Rhymes and Rhyming Poems, and Tongue Twisters

Songs, nursery rhymes and rhyming poems, and tongue twisters have been part of early childhood education for centuries, but only in recent decades have we come to understand more fully how they support literacy development. It is amazing how many opportunities these old favorites offer for building phonological awareness. Being aware of these opportunities and putting them into action in your classroom will help you develop important skills in children.

Songs

Most young children love to sing. It's fun. Singing also develops musical skills such as pitch and rhythm, and it builds cultural literacy. For instance, songs like "Take Me out to the Ballgame" and "We Shall Overcome" contain important lessons about our country and its history. Singing also builds phonological awareness, especially the abilities to recognize rhyming words, generate rhyming words, and move sounds around to create new words (skills 2, 3, and 8 on page 92).

Recognizing and Generating Rhyming Words

So many songs for young children contain rhyming words, for example "Twinkle, Twinkle, Little Star":

> Twinkle, twinkle, little star
> How I wonder what you are
> Up above the world so high
> Like a diamond in the sky
> Twinkle, twinkle little star
> How I wonder what you are

Or more modern songs such as "Three Green and Speckled Frogs":

> Three green and speckled frogs
> Sitting on a speckled log
> Eating some most delicious bugs – Yum! Yum!
> One jumped into the pool
> Where it was nice and cool
> Now there are two green speckled frogs – Ribbit! Ribbit!
> (and so on for two to one and one to none)

After singing together, you may want to read aloud *Five Green and Speckled Frogs* by Priscilla Burris (2003), a picture-book version of the song.

Singing these songs to infants sets the stage for building phonological awareness. But you should help toddlers and young preschoolers learn to sing the songs themselves. With older preschoolers, focus on the rhyming words or "words that have ending parts that sound the same." You can identify the rhyming words for them or see if they can pick out the words themselves.

Some songs provide opportunities for children to generate rhyming words for example, "Down by the Bay":

> Down by the bay
> Where the watermelons grow
> Back to my home
> I dare not go
> For if I do
> My mother will say
> Have you ever seen _____ wearing _____
> Down by the bay

Have the children help you fill in the blanks with rhyming words, such as *a cat/a hat* or *some ants/some pants*. Alternative versions include

> Have you ever seen a _____ eating a _____
>
> Have you even seen a _____ walk with a _____

"Have you even seen a _____ walk with a _____" may be a good one to start with because the potential for sensible word pairs is greater compared with the other two fill-in passages—for example, *dog/frog, duck/truck*, and *ape/grape*. The possibilities are virtually endless! That said, when we sing songs like these with children, we do not insist on real words for the second blank. The children may sing, for example, "Have you ever seen a *horse* eating a *lorse!*" Not only is this use of nonsense words hysterically funny to most of them, it suggests they are using the skill of generating rhymes rather than just memorizing word pairs they have heard before. It is important to point out, though, that these are "silly words" that don't mean anything, especially if you work with English-language learners who may be confused by the mix of words they know and these unfamiliar-sounding words.

As we suggested for "Three Green and Speckled Frogs," you may want to accompany this activity with a Read Aloud. "Down by the Bay" is the basis of a book of the same name by Raffi, illustrated by Nadine Westcott (1987).

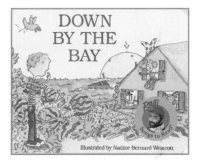

Moving Sounds Around to Create New Words

Moving sounds around is a difficult skill for most young children. So it's comforting to know that there are many songs that can provide them with fun practice.

One well-known song, "The Name Game" (see box at right), not only helps you address the skill of moving sounds around to create new words, but also helps you address other skills such as generating words that start with the same sound and blending sounds into words.

Singing this song takes practice, but we have seen even young 3-year-olds do it. Children younger than that may enjoy hearing you sing it.

The Name Game

Shirley!

Shirley, Shirley bo Birley
Bonana fanna fo Firley

Mee my mo Mirley, Shirley!

Lincoln!

Lincoln, Lincoln bo Bincoln
Bonana fanna fo Fincoln

Mee my mo Mincoln, Lincoln!

Arnold!

Arnold, Arnold bo Barnold
Bonana fanna fo Farnold

Mee my mo Marnold, Arnold!

"Apples and Bananas" is another song that requires moving sounds around, and it may be a little less challenging than "The Name Game" because the same ten sounds are always used. They are the long vowel sounds (/ā/ as in *ape*, /ē/ as in *eagle*, /ī/ as in *ice*, /ō/ as in *open*, /ū/ as in *unicorn*) and the short vowel sounds (/ă/ as in *apple*, /ĕ/ as in *egg*, /ĭ/ as in *igloo*, /ŏ/ as in *octopus*, /ŭ/ as in *upside-down*).

> I like to ēat, ēat, ēat, apples and bananas (repeat)
>
> I like to āet, āet, āet, āpples and banānās (repeat)
>
> I like to ēat, ēat, ēat, ēeples and banēenēes (repeat)
>
> I like to īet, īet, īet, īepples and banīenīes (repeat)
>
> (and so on for the rest of the long vowel and short vowel sounds)

"Old MacDonald" can be adapted similarly. As with "Apples and Bananas," this version of "Old MacDonald" encourages children to move sounds around to create new words and helps develop other skills such as generating words that start with the same sound. Instead of just singing

> Old MacDonald had a farm
>
> E – I – E – I – O...

sing

> Old MacDonald had a farm
>
> LE – LI – LE – LI – LO
>
> And on this farm he had an /l/ [the sound, not the letter]
>
> LE – LI – LE – LI – LO
>
> With a /l/ /l/ here and a /l/ /l/ there
>
> Here a /l/, there a /l/, everywhere a /l/, /l/
>
> Old MacDonald had a /l/
>
> LE – LI – LE – LI – LO
>
> (and so on for different sounds)

A favorite song in early childhood settings that requires moving sounds around and other phonological awareness skills is "Willoughby Wallaby Woo."

> Willoughby wallaby woo
>
> An elephant sat on you
>
> Willoughby wallaby wee
>
> An elephant sat on me
>
> Willoughby wallaby Wavid
>
> An elephant sat on David
>
> Willoughby wallaby Weisha
>
> An elephant sat on Keisha
>
> (and so on for the different names in the class)

As explained in chapter 8, children's names are extremely useful in developing literacy, and they provide great fodder for word play in songs, as illustrated above. We encourage you, though, to ask children for permission to use their names. Some children may feel uncomfortable with using their names for such purposes.

There are countless Mother Goose nursery rhyme books. We especially like this version, The Neighborhood Mother Goose by Nina Crews (2004), which helps children understand the rhymes by placing characters in familiar, modern settings. We also like Father Gander's Nursery Rhymes: The Equal Rhymes Amendment (Father Gander, 1986), which pairs traditional rhymes with updated, gender-neutral versions.

Nursery Rhymes and Rhyming Poems

Nursery rhymes and rhyming poems offer many of the same opportunities for phonological awareness development as songs do. Not only do they contain many wonderful rhyming words and passages, but they often contain wordplay that young children find amusing. Also, some rhymes and poems are so ingrained in our cultural literacy that we would be doing children a disservice by *not* teaching them. Consider, for example, how often the image of the cow jumping over the moon is found.

Recognizing and Generating Rhyming Words

By definition, nursery rhymes contain lots of rich, clever rhyming words and phrases.

> Little Miss Muffet
> Sat on her tuffet
> Eating her curds and whey
> Along came a spider
> And sat down beside her
> And frightened Miss Muffet away

More modern nursery rhymes also contain them. Consider *Miss Mary Mack Mack Mack, all dressed in black black black.*

Shel Silverstein, Jack Prelutsky, and many other contemporary children's poets make extensive use of rhyming in their work. And many children's picture books are written in rhyme. We love *Is Your Mama a Llama?* (Guarino, 1989) in part because the book encourages children to use knowledge of rhyme to help guess the animal.

> "Is your mama a llama?" I asked my friend Dave.
> "No, she is not," is the answer Dave gave.
> "She hangs by her feet, and she lives in a cave. I do not believe that's how llamas behave."
> "Oh," I said. "You are right about that. I think your mama sounds more like a . . ."
> [Turn the page.]
> "Bat!"

We read nursery rhymes, poems, and simple rhyming books to children beginning at their infancy and continuing through preschool. When children hear favorite rhymes over and over again, they may memorize them and, from there, participate in phonological awareness activities like the one described in the next section.

Moving Sounds Around to Create New Words

Many preschoolers love to make silly versions of well-known rhymes. For example, they might substitute a /r/ for the first sound in each word in "Little Miss Muffet."

> Rittle Riss Ruffet
>
> Rat ron rer ruffet
>
> Reating rer rurds rand rhey
>
> Ralong rame a rider
>
> Rand rat rown reside rer
>
> Rand rightened Riss Ruffet raway!

Imagine how funny many children find this activity. Be creative, knowing that you're building phonological awareness skills. Give children lots of opportunities to practice these rhymes in a no-pressure, fun atmosphere.

Tongue Twisters

Tongue twisters are great for helping children recognize and generate words that start with the same sound (part of skills 4 and 5 in the list on page 92). There are many tongue twisters, some you may already know (such as *Peter Piper picked a peck of pickled peppers* and *She sells seashells down by the seashore*, which uses two sounds, /sh/ and /s/) and some that may be new, like the one to the right. For a

Tongue twisters provide a fun way to help develop phonological awareness. This one, from Six Sick Sheep: 101 Tongue Twisters *(Cole & Calmenson, 1993), contains /sh/ and /s/ words.*

Shelly shouldn't shake saltshakers, should she?

whole book of them, check out *Six Sick Sheep: 101 Tongue Twisters* by Joanna Cole and Stephanie Calmenson (1993).

Do not assume that children will realize that many words within a tongue twister begin with the same sound. Explicitly point out that fact, perhaps by identifying the letter or letters associated with the sound and stretching out the sound as described in the last section of this chapter.

Writing new tongue twisters with children helps them learn to generate words that begin with the same sound. Start by reading or saying some tongue twisters so that children understand how they're constructed. Then give them a starter to create a new tongue twister, such as one of their first names and an apt adjective. (Notice the opportunity for vocabulary instruction too.)

> " *Writing new tongue twisters with children helps them learn to generate words that begin with the same sound. Start by reading or saying some tongue twisters so that children understand how they're constructed.* "

Magical Mario . . .

Prince Paul . . .

Silly Steven . . .

Elegant Emily . . .

Repeating the target sound multiple times and/or giving an engaging, inspirational category will help children come up with words to complete the tongue twister. For example, after giving them the starter "Magical Mario . . . ," you might repeat the /m/ sound and give the category foods. Children might then say "macaroni," "meatballs," and "milk." From there, work with them to assemble the words into a tongue twister:

Magical Mario must make macaroni, meatballs, and milk!

To further develop awareness of the sounds in the self-created tongue twister, write it out and illustrate it with children's drawings, magazine pictures, and/or photographs and post it in the room. You might also want to consider reading *Potluck* by Anne Shelby (1991) at the start of this activity, which tells the story of a class potluck party in which each child brings a food that starts with the same letter or letters as his or her name.

Word Games

We want children to play with language. The activities we've discussed thus far can certainly help them do that, and so can word games. Word games are especially good for addressing phonological awareness skills. In this section we describe a few games to get you started, but feel free to make up your own!

"Count the Beats!"

(to build skills in separating words into syllables or beats, skill 1 in the list on page 92.)

In this game, which is appropriate for preschoolers and some older toddlers, the class sorts itself based on the number of beats or syllables in children's names. You might have all the children with one-beat names, such as Ben and Grace, stand up, then have all of the children with two-beat names, such as Rosa and David, jump up and down, and so on. Or you might put toys on the floor and work with children to sort the toys by the number of beats in their names—doll, truck, block; puzzle, baseball, teddy; and so forth.

As children organize themselves and/or toys into beat categories, have them break words into syllables by clapping their hands or patting their legs as they shout out each name. Movements like this make the task easier for children because it makes it more concrete. We have also found that it helps if you model breaking words into syllables for children while saying them, as in "pa-per," "pen-cil," and so forth.

As with any learning task, children develop their ability to break words into syllables at different rates. Some children will need a lot of practice and support from you, and some may not. You may want to do this activity in small, mixed-ability groups so that each group has a few children who can model for others.

"Going on Vacation"

(to build skills in separating words into syllables or beats, generating rhymes, and generating words that start with the same sound—skills 1, 3, and 5 in the list on page 92—and other aspects of phonological awareness.)

In this game, older preschoolers take turns announcing something they will take on vacation that begins with the same sound. For example, you might start with "I'm going on vacation and I'm going to take a ball." The first child needs to think of something else to take on vacation that starts with /b/, such as a bear or barrette. One by one, the children repeat the "I'm going on vacation and I'm going to take a" stem and announce an item until each child has had a turn. From there, move to another sound and repeat the process. An alternate way to play this game is to have each child list everything others have said before announcing his or her item, but we believe this is too difficult for most preschoolers.

An easier alternative is to have children come up with items that have the same number of syllables (for example, suitcase, raincoat, sunscreen) or that rhyme. If you choose rhymes, be sure to start with a word that rhymes with a lot of other words, such as *log* or *pan*. Otherwise, children will get frustrated by their lack of choices. Experiment to see which versions work with your children.

"Who Gets Up?"

(to build all phonological awareness skills listed on page 92.)

In the early childhood setting, it's usually best to have children move from one activity to the next in a staggered fashion, rather than all at once, so that children aren't overwhelmed by the crowd. And phonological awareness can be a part of this process. In "Who Gets Up?" you have clusters of children move according to sounds in their names. For example, you might call all the children whose names start with /j/ to get up. Remember, to build phonological awareness, it's important to say the *sound*, not the letter name. So, when you call out /j/, Genevieve should get up, along with Justin and Jocelyn. If this is confusing to children, explain that two different letters can stand for /j/—*j* and *g*.

You can also do a rhyming version of "Who Gets Up?" by calling all the children whose names rhyme with a particular word such as *still*. Bill, Will, and Phil would stand up. Or you may have children blend the sounds in the name as you call it out—/w/ /o/ /n/ (Juan) for example. By carrying out these variations, you make the game work well for children at different levels by highlighting different skills. Some children may be called by the first sound in their name, others by a rhyming word, others by sound segments.

Playing word games is an entertaining, time-efficient way to promote phonological awareness skills. Building just a few into your weekly plans may have great results.

Stretching Words

Stretching words involves slowing down pronunciation to emphasize the sounds in words—such as saying "mmmmm-oooooooommmmmmmm" for "mom." This strategy may pale in excitement in comparison to those we've suggested so far, but it is important because it can help children isolate and recognize sounds and groups of sounds in words, which is essential to developing phonological awareness.

Sounds that you can say continuously are easiest to stretch and are commonly represented by the letters *a*, *c* (as in celery), *e*, *f*, *h*, *i*, *l*, *m*, *n*, *o*, *r*, *s*, *u*, *v*, *w*, *y*, and *z*. Sounds you cannot say continuously are more difficult to stretch. These are the sounds commonly represented by *b*, *c* (as in cat), *d*, *g*, *j*, *k*, *p*, *q*, *t*, and *x*. So, when teaching these sounds, we repeat the sound multiple times for the children, as in "/b/ /b/ /b/ ball."

Do not overly distort the sounds when you stretch words. And be sure to keep the sound in the context of the word. That is, try to say the sound the way it sounds in that particular word, and follow it with the rest of that word. Although we emphasize the importance of picking out individual sounds in words, we must remember that those sounds aren't meant to be separated and, therefore, may vary a bit. For example, the /f/ in *fish* is slightly different from the /f/ in *fat* because the vowels have a

Eleven Enriching Books for Building Phonological Awareness

Book List

Separating words into syllables or beats

Nearly any book works well for this, especially those with a strong rhythm, for example:

Silly Sally by Audrey Wood. Harcourt, 1992

We're Going on a Bear Hunt by Michael Rosen. Illustrated by Helen Oxenbury. Margaret K. McElderry Books, 1989

Recognizing and/or generating rhyming words

There are so many books to develop this skill! We made ourselves stop at six.

Duck in the Truck by Jez Alborough. HarperCollins, 2000

Hop on Pop by Dr. Seuss. Random House, 1963

Is Your Mama a Llama? by Deborah Guarino. Illustrated by Steven Kellogg. Scholastic, 1989

Room on the Broom by Julia Donaldson. Illustrated by Axel Scheffler. Scholastic, 2001

Toes Have Wiggles Kids Have Giggles by Harriet Ziefert. Illustrated by Rebecca Doughty. G. P. Putnam and Sons, 2002

Recognizing words that start with the same sound

Again, many books work well for this, including the alphabet books listed in chapter 4. Also consider

Sheep in a Shop by Nancy Shaw. Illustrated by Margot Apple. Houghton Mifflin, 1997

Moving sounds around to create new words

Ook the Book and Other Silly Rhymes by Lissa Rovetch. Illustrated by Shannon McNeill. Chronicle Books, 2001

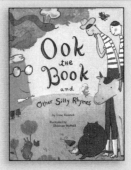

Runny Babbit: A Billy Sook by Shel Silverstein. HarperCollins, 2005

There's a Wocket in My Pocket by Dr. Seuss. Random House, 1974

slight influence on the sound. Children need practice picking out sounds in spite of this influence.

One of the best times to stretch words with children is when they ask how to spell a word—in other words, when they are trying to figure out what letter a word begins or ends with, or what letters go in between the first one and last one. Stretching words while you read or write in front of children, even toddlers, is also a good idea. For example, you might sometimes stretch the beginning sounds of children's names when reading or writing those names or calling out who will play in the block area.

As children develop phonological awareness, adjust your degree of stretching. For example, while you might say "mmmm-ooooommmmm" initially, later you might only need to say "mmoomm." Then "m o m," emphasizing each sound, and eventually "mom" naturally.

Concluding Thoughts

Children's ability to hear and process the sounds in words is critical to their later success at figuring out unfamiliar words. When an adult asks a beginning reader to "sound it out," he or she will see better results if the reader has had years of practice in hearing and blending the sounds in words. We have countless opportunities to support children's phonological awareness in the early childhood years through play. We hope you'll try some of the ideas in this chapter. Sounds like fun!

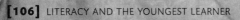

CHAPTER 6

Dramatic Play and Literacy

"Let's play 'work'," 3-year-old Violet announces to no one in particular.

She then begins to tap on the computer with the rhythm of an experienced

typist. She pauses to answer a phone only she hears ring. Switching the

phone to her left shoulder, she grabs a pencil and makes marks onto a

nearby notepad. She ends her call with "Thanks. Have a great day!"

There is nothing exceptional about Violet's play except that it is supported by materials such as a computer, phone, paper, and pencil and by encouragement from her mother, Susan, who uses those materials every day in her work. You probably see play like this happening in your own classroom and are wondering if there are ways to enhance it. By the time you finish this chapter, we think you'll answer yes. In this chapter we

- describe the development of dramatic play.
- explain the value of dramatic play.
- provide examples of research on the role of dramatic play in supporting literacy.
- offer ideas for designing dramatic play experiences that promote literacy.

The Value of Dramatic Play

Okay, we confess. Dramatic play is one of our favorite topics. No other area of the classroom allows children to be as creative or to explore so many new ideas as a well-designed dramatic play area. Children can spend time as paleontologists hunting for fossils one week and as deep-sea explorers the next. The abandon children exhibit while engaged in dramatic play is enthralling.

Of course, dramatic play doesn't happen only in the area designated for it. The block area may become an elaborate highway system, with children taking on different roles. Some might be architects designing buildings, others might be truck drivers dropping off materials, and still others might be construction

The Continuum of Dramatic Play

Children are wired to learn about and act upon the world around them from a very early age. Babies watch the facial expressions and listen to the sounds of adults and go on to imitate them. As they gain control of their motor skills, they use toys to pretend to do things they see adults doing. You have probably seen a 1-year-old holding a play phone to his ear and babbling into it. Although he has no words yet, he sounds like he is having a conversation. He pauses, expresses emotions, and raises his voice at the ends of phrases as if asking a question. Children imitate our tones as well as our words and gestures.

As children's vocabulary grows, they incorporate new words into their play. At this phase, it's best to support their play by including realistic props, such as toy phones and dishes. Their play is quite literal and a reenactment of what they have seen in their environment.

Increasingly, pretend play becomes more imaginative and complex. When children are better able to make up their own play, they start to use more abstract props, such as a block as the phone. While children still imitate adult roles and events they hear about in books, they start to add their own spin on things. A child might pretend to

be a superhero with amazing powers. She might use those powers to save a baby at the zoo or extinguish a fire at the campsite. Neither of those settings are known for containing superheroes. In the child's mind, though, sometimes superheroes just show up. When children use their imaginations in their play, ask them what props they need and what materials they need to create those props. By providing open-ended materials such as paper, markers, and clipboards, we support a wide range of literacy play. Who knows, Super Reader may come to the rescue!

workers building the highway. Dramatic play is important no matter where it occurs because it allows children to

- experiment with familiar and unfamiliar roles, which helps them reinforce and consolidate their knowledge. Younger children usually take on family roles such as parent and child (Garvey & Berndt, 1977), whereas older children are more likely to experiment by taking on job roles such as doctor or cashier. Taking a field trip to a hospital or grocery store, where children can see real people in these roles, can enhance this play. (See chapter 10 for more on weaving literacy into field trips.)

- work through issues that are troubling them. Older preschoolers create or re-create fictional characters that help them grapple with issues they find frightening or uncontrollable (Kostelnik, Whiren, & Stein, 1986). For example, a child might be a superhero protecting someone from a bully or a knight fighting a dragon.

- play with concepts and ideas to make them their own. For example, a child may gain understandings about birds by pretending to be a bird in a nest.

- build literacy in ways that other classroom activities do not.

Photo: Alison Billman

Top: *In the flower shop, children develop writing skills, math skills, and their knowledge of natural science.*

Bottom: *A climber is converted to a lively post office where children can prepare and deliver messages they've written in the writing center.*

DRAMATIC PLAY THEMES AND PROPS	LITERACY PROPS
SUBMARINE large piece of cardboard (appliance box cut open) with portholes cut in side, steering wheel, periscope, pictures of fish or other underwater creatures, blue tulle or crepe paper draped from ceiling, green crepe paper draped from ceiling for seaweed, diving masks, flippers	Guidebooks on fish, informational books on underwater life like Under the Sea (Delafosse & Gallimard, 1999), posters with text about life underwater
ICE CREAM PARLOR dishes, cones made from paper, spoons, table and chairs, tubs of "ice cream" (yarn pom-poms in a variety of colors), ice cream scoops, money, cash register, aprons	Order forms and pencils, poster of flavor choices, price poster, store sign, labels on flavor buckets, empty containers of chocolate sauce, butterscotch, or cherry toppings
FIREHOUSE phone, hoses, fire truck created from box, climber, or lined-up chairs, coats, rubber boots, fire hats, extinguisher (can be oatmeal can covered in red paper with piece of hose attached)	Map of city, poster of the order in which to put on gear, fire safety posters, paper and pencil for taking phone messages
FLOWER SHOP texture table with potting soil, plastic pots, artificial flowers, phone, cash register, money, shovels, plastic vases, refrigerator for floral arrangements, ribbon	Seed packets with labels, posters of plants, FTD book (get an old one from your local florist), FTD calendar (free from florist), sticks with names of plants on them, order forms and pencils
BAKERY flour in texture table, natural colored play dough (and tons of it!), cookie cutters, rolling pins, pans, oven, sink, aprons, oven mitts, phone, cash register, money, boxes decorated to look like cakes	Bakery sign, price lists, labels on shelves of baked goods, order forms, pencils, recipe cards, cookbook, paper for children to label their creations
PIZZA PARLOR felt circles of white and red to make pizza and sauce, felt toppings such as cheese, pepperoni, mushrooms, green pepper (each in their own container for sorting), oven, oven mitts, phone, cash register, money, table for eating "in," dishes, apron	Order forms, pencils, pizza cookbook, menus, signs advertising the daily special

OTHER THEMES Other themes include bookshop, zoo, spaceship, train, and baby hospital. You might also try ideas inspired by a Read Aloud. For example, Susan once put a children's pool filled with straw in her dramatic play area. After reading *Make Way for Ducklings* (McCloskey, 1941), the children reenacted that story. At one point, a little girl stood up and announced, "I can't fly... I'm molting!" The dramatic play area became a forum for retelling, chewing on the ideas in the text, and further comprehending them. Regardless of what inspires themes, dramatic play areas can contribute to children's literacy if they are designed with literacy in mind.

How Does Dramatic Play Support Literacy?

Dramatic play supports literacy in many ways. In this section, we discuss some of them.

Dramatic Play Allows Children to Experiment With Purposes for Literacy

By including functional print such as newspapers, letters from family members, menus, shelf signs, coupons, and food containers with recognizable logos and names, we create an environment that allows children to interact with print as they see others do. They see firsthand that there are many ways to use text, which is very different from what they see during group time, where we tend to read mostly books. Researchers Susan Neuman and Kathleen Roskos (1993b) found that classrooms rich in both functional print and Read Aloud books inspired more literacy-focused dramatic play and resulted in children having greater literacy competencies.

> *By including functional print such as newspapers, letters from family members, menus, shelf signs, coupons, and food containers with recognizable logos and names, we create an environment that allows children to interact with print as they see others do.*

Photo: Annie Moses

By adding menus to the housekeeping dramatic play area, the classroom can become a restaurant.

Dramatic Play Allows Children to See That Different Tasks Require Different Texts

As literacy props change with theme, children see that different tasks require different texts. For example, the firefighter might need a map of the city, but the veterinarian needs an appointment book and test results for someone's pet cat. The restaurant contains menus, but the flower shop contains seed packets and a chart on how plants grow. Exposing children to a wide range of texts not only helps them understand the various purposes of text, but also helps them differentiate features of text.

Dramatic Play Allows Children to Produce a Wide Variety of Texts

By exposing children to a wide variety of functional texts, we encourage them to create many kinds of text—not just stories. This is important because we need to develop children's knowledge of a wide range of genres. (See chapters 1 and 2.) Children may make traffic signs for the block area, a shopping list for the grocery store, an order form and receipt at the restaurant, a letter to a friend to mail at the post office, or storage labels for materials in all play areas.

> *Exposing children to a wide range of texts not only helps them understand the various purposes of text, but also helps them differentiate features of text.*

A child fills out a registration form while playing auto shop as another child takes an adult's order while playing restaurant.

Prop Boxes (a.k.a. Dramatic Play Kits): How Do I Decide What to Include?

Prop boxes, or containers for the materials listed in the box on pages 111 to 112, have been shown to enhance children's literacy skills (Neuman & Roskos, 1993b). Creating them is simple: Use an empty box for the props according to theme, such as restaurant menus for a food theme or seed packets for a flower-shop theme. Of course the box would also contain other props such as, for a flower-shop theme, silk flowers, plastic pots, trowels. While many early childhood suppliers charge quite a bit for kits like these, you can come up with dramatic play kits on your own just by letting your themes guide you. Regardless of your theme, keep in mind the following criteria when assembling prop boxes:

Appropriateness

- Are the materials safe for children? (Avoid using items that might be construed as dangerous, such as play razors, plastic bags, or lead pencils.)
- Do the materials support your theme?
- Can children identify the theme just by looking at the props?

Authenticity

- Do the materials represent things a child might find in the real world?
- Can you locate "real" materials such as menus from a restaurant or message pads from an office?

Creativity

- Can the materials be used in a variety of ways?
- Are there ways for the children to contribute to the box? Could they create appropriate materials themselves?
- Do you have a variety of materials for each kit that appeal to different children? For example, in a fire station prop box, you might include not only firefighter hats and hoses, but dolls and a typewriter to spur imaginative play.
- Do you have a variety of kits to attract different children to the area? For example, some children will never go into "housekeeping" but will be very attracted to a bakery. Similar but different themes.

Connectedness to text

- Are the materials connected to a text that you have used? Can you provide a copy of that text in the box? (Keep in mind that not all texts are books. Some are lists, menus, songs, etc.)
- Have you read related texts to the children or will you provide them as a reference that they might use in the center on their own (such as a guidebook in a campout)? If you include a reference book, do you plan to spend time in the center helping children use the book?
- If the text is environmental (such as ice cream parlor signs), how will you help children read and make sense of it?

Usefulness

- Will children actually use the materials? Would a demonstration help them to see the materials' usefulness?

Variety

- Do you have enough kits to change your themes every week or so? (Some programs leave materials out longer because their children don't come every day or because they observe continued interest and growth in the play in that area.)
- Are you representing a range of themes that may appeal to all your children over time? For example, having only transportation-related themes, such as boat, airplane, or submarine, may appeal to some children but not others. Conversely, only nurturing themes like hospital, housekeeping, vet clinic may appeal to a completely different group. Select and vary themes to cover all your children's interests.

Once you have thought of the kits you desire, send a note to parents asking for materials. Tell them the theme and see what they send. You may be surprised by their resourcefulness and desire to help you enrich your classroom. In your note, be sure to mention that your aim is to help their children become more in tune with the print in their world as well as provide opportunities for them to learn the many purposes of literacy. Reach out to your community and explain what you are doing. Everyone will be excited.

"Did you read the sign?" Clean-up and five-minute signs give literacy-based warnings that a transition is coming.

limit the number of children. We suggest no more than four children in the area at a time. That way, children can hear one another speak and share materials easily. This number also allows enough space for you to drop in to facilitate play, mediate conflicts, and simply enjoy the interactions.

use literacy for clean up. In addition to using a five-minute sign and a clean-up sign (which are discussed in chapter 11), be sure to label shelves and containers in the dramatic play area for easy clean up. For example, in a grocery store, the children might sort materials by vegetables, boxed goods, dairy, and so on to put them away. Cleaning up this way promotes vocabulary development, interaction with text, and cooperation around a literacy task. All good things!

be open to new uses for props. Children's play may move in a direction that you may not anticipate. That's okay. Go with it because they may be playing out something that they have observed before that can enrich the play. Also, let children bring props into the dramatic play area from other areas or create their own props to extend the play. When Susan set up a campsite in her dramatic play area, one little guy left the area and went to the art area to construct binoculars from two toilet paper tubes and tape. He brought them back to the dramatic play area, announced he was bird-watching, and spent the rest of his time watching for birds and looking them up in a guidebook. Let's face it, sometimes kids can invent better props than we can provide. Or they think of things we don't. Honor their ideas. If you do, their play will mean more to them.

Concluding Thoughts

While some of you may be excited to try out the ideas in this chapter, some of you may be daunted by everything you need to do to get dramatic play going. No doubt, if you have no dramatic play kits now, you have work to do! The good news is you only have to assemble one box every week or every other week (depending on how long you leave a kit out). Consider teaming up with a colleague to create kits. That way, it will take half the time to develop your dramatic play collection. Over time, you will assemble a wonderful collection of materials that will help your children develop not only their literacy skills, but also their sense of themselves. It is certainly a worthy investment.

Five Great Books to Support Early Pretending

From Head to Toe
by Eric Carle. HarperFestival, 1999

I'm as Quick as a Cricket
by Audrey Wood. Illustrated by Don Wood. Child's Play, 1998

Pretend You're a Cat
by Jean Marzollo. Illustrated by Jerry Pinkney. Puffin, 1997

Teddy Bear, Teddy Bear: A Classic Action Rhyme
illustrated by Michael Hague. Morrow Junior Books, 1993

The Wheels on the Bus
by Paul O. Zelinsky. Penguin Putnam, 1990

Five Great Books to Support Later Pretending

Big Red Barn by Margaret Wise Brown. Illustrated by Felicia Bond. HarperFestival, 1994

Caps for Sale
by Esphyr Slobodkina. HaperCollins, 1975

Goldilocks and the Three Bears
by James Marshall. Penguin Putnam, 1997

The Treasure
by Uri Shulevitz. Farrar, Straus & Giroux, 1986

The Very Hungry Caterpillar
by Eric Carle. Philomel Books, 1994

easily and feel secure in it when perusing and enjoying good books and other reading materials on their own or with friends. With the right setup and materials, children will have enough space to sit down, get comfortable, and become engaged.

Why Have One? The Benefits of a Book Nook

The importance of having books available in child-care settings cannot be overstated. Here are three research-supported benefits of books nooks:

Book Nooks Foster Knowledge About Print and the Uses of Literacy

> " *In the book nook, you can demonstrate how we read books, why we read books, and what we gain from reading books.* "

When you share a book with a child, you support his or her emergent literacy in a powerful way (Neuman, 1999). In the book nook, you can demonstrate how we read books, why we read books, and what we gain from reading books. You also support literacy learning by allowing children to decide what texts to read, to turn the pages, and to pretend-read by encouraging them to create their own stories to go along with the illustrations. All of these activities familiarize children with print and help them see literacy's usefulness.

Book Nooks Promote Vocabulary

Exposure to books, as well as quality interactions between adults and children around books, has been found to promote vocabulary growth. For instance, David Dickinson and Miriam Smith (1994) found that the quality of talk around books between preschoolers and their teachers had an impact on those children's receptive vocabulary development. Preschoolers whose teachers engage them in high-quality talk tended to have larger receptive vocabularies at the end of kindergarten than those who didn't. (Receptive vocabulary are words that children can understand when they hear or read them but do not necessarily use in their own speech).

Photo: Alison Billman

Book Nooks Motivate Children to Read

Providing opportunities to engage with books on a regular basis can increase children's motivation and desire to read throughout their lives (Morrow, 2002). Children who have early experiences with print tend to read earlier and enjoy reading more (for example, Dickinson & Smith, 1994; Neuman et al., 2001).

The book nook is a great location to experience reading. Help children think about all the different times when they can visit it, for instance, during free-choice time, after snack or outdoor time, before the start of a new activity, and while you are working with small groups.

When a book nook is well planned and inviting, children are more likely to use it. In one study, children chose to spend more time in the book nook after it had been transformed into a more appealing, literacy-rich space (Morrow & Weinstein, 1986). Lesley Morrow and Carol Weinsten made sure that books and book covers were displayed prominently, postings were hung that encouraged children to read, a wider variety of reading materials

Providing a wide range of texts will spark the interests of all children and entice them to read.

" *Exposure to books, as well as quality interactions between adults and children around books, has been found to promote vocabulary growth.* "

Stocking the Nook With Great Books

There are many things to consider when stocking a book nook with reading materials. Here are some considerations:

Choose Enough Books

Given all of the benefits of book nooks, it is surprising to find that many early-child-care settings do not have them. In a study of 30 day-care centers, researchers found books or book areas in only nine of them (Dunn, Beach, & Kontos, 1994). Experts recommend at least five to eight books per child in early childhood settings. However, many early-child-care centers fall

Flannel Boards: Interactive Storytelling

Flannel boards can promote language and literacy. You can either buy one at a teacher store or an educational-toy store or create one by gluing a large felt piece to a wooden board, cork-board, or piece of heavy card-board. (Susan has even used an old flannel pillow case over a piece of plywood cut to size.) Be sure the board is propped on a slant so that felt characters and other objects stay on. Cut characters and other objects for stories from felt and decorate them. Or draw or photocopy characters and other objects onto paper, cut them out, decorate them, protect them by laminating them or seal-ing them in clear contact paper, and glue felt strips to the back of them so they stick to the board.

Commercially made sets are avail-able from sources such as http://www.teachchildren.com or http://www.homespun kids.com.

From there, bring stories alive through interactive story-telling by you and your children. Specifically, as you tell your whole group a story such as "Goldilocks and the Three Bears," act it out on the flannel board using cutouts of Goldilocks, the bears, bowls for porridge, etc. Then, make the flannel board and cutouts available to children so they can do their own retelling of the story you told and, perhaps, other favorite stories. By doing this, children learn story struc-ture, build oral communication skills, and acquire book language and vocabulary.

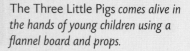

The Three Little Pigs *comes alive in the hands of young children using a flannel board and props.*

short of that amount. In a survey study of 318 early childhood centers in 36 states, 28 percent of centers tended to have fewer than one book for each child, according to the directors who filled out the survey (Neuman et al., 2001).

So one of the first things you can do is to stock up on books for your setting! Once you have them, put some on display and make them available for use. You may not want to put out all the books all the time, because too many can be overwhelming. We recommend displaying a few titles at a time and rotating them at least weekly. A good formula for determining how many books to display at once is two times the number of children allowed in the area at a time. For example, if four children are allowed in the area, display eight books on the shelf. The rest of the titles can be on shelves, in tubs or baskets, or otherwise available.

Choose High-Quality, Developmentally Appropriate Books

The quality of the texts should always be a factor in deciding what to include in a book nook. You should also consider the ages of the children in your setting and choose books that are typically appropriate for children at those ages.

Beware of mass-market books. Although they tend to be inexpensive and widely available at the grocery, wholesale, and discount stores, we strongly advise that you screen them carefully for quality. These books are often based on television shows and movies (rather than an author and illustrator's unique vision) or are part of a large series of books that are highly formulaic, and the quality of writing and illustrations tends to be low. Having a few mass-market books on hand is all right, since children will recognize and might enjoy stories about their favorite characters. However, too many—more than 10 percent of your whole collection—is not okay. Children need exposure to quality contemporary literature, classic tales, and reliable and engaging informational texts—all with beautiful illustrations and well-written text.

Here are more specific guidelines to follow when evaluating books for quality and appropriateness:

Number of Words Are there lots of words on each page? Are there large illustrations with little print? Very few? Do the illustrations dominate ... or does the text? Consider the ages and developmental levels of the children in your setting as you evaluate the answers to these questions. One of the reasons board books are so infant friendly is because they contain very few words.

Artwork and Language Since most children will be "reading" only the pictures, selecting books with rich illustrations and excellent photos is important. So include books with rich artwork and quality photographs for children to discuss and draw meaning from. Additionally, read aloud books with rich language and then place in them in the book nook for children to revisit.

Topic Select books on topics that are familiar to the children. That way, the children will be able to use what they know to make sense of the material. Get to know your children's interests and find books that complement them.

Photo: Marcel Charpentier

- engaging with books and other reading materials on their own in a comfortable spot.

- observing others interacting with reading materials.

- using the flannel board to retell a favorite story.

- sharing something they have written with a friend or an adult.

- using the listening center.

- reading the posters.

- finding out something about the theme in a related book.

- locating all the letters in their names in an alphabet book.

- finding the colors they are wearing in a color book.

- finding the book you read to the group last week.

Provide opportunities for infants to explore books. This will begin a love of learning that is sure to last. Remember to give infants reading materials that will withstand explorations.

Also, when you are introducing the book nook, you can discuss guidelines for using it, including respecting the materials in it and behaving acceptably.

Value the Book Nook

Just as you probably reinforce the importance of clean up after play and hand washing after bathroom breaks, you should reinforce the importance of reading. You can do this by spending time in the book nook with children and talking directly with them about how you find and use a book. You can also demonstrate good reading behavior by sitting alongside children and catching up (briefly) on some professional development reading as they catch up on some reading of their own. This will demonstrate your love of reading as well as the usefulness of books.

"Check Out" Books

Make the book nook a resource for enhancing and informing play in other areas of the classroom. While in the dramatic play area, for example, a child may go to the book nook to find an informational text about firefighters to see what firefighters wear and do at work. Children may remember an informational book that talks about how caterpillars turn into butterflies and use it to explore the caterpillars in the science center. When working with children in other centers, remind them that the book nook is likely to contain helpful resources and show them a few examples.

Offer Literacy Activities

You can increase participation in the book nook by introducing new activities on a regular basis. For instance, you can ask a question such as "What do you like to do with your family?" during large group time and then have another adult record children's answers during choice time on a chart in the book nook. Also, the book nook is a great location for showcasing materials produced in the writing center. For example, consider having your children write an "All About Me" book in which they paste pictures of themselves, their family members, favorite places, and things to do. Stock the writing center with needed materials—paper, writing utensils, and binding materials—and offer a helping hand. You can create slips of paper with sentences such as "My birthday is _____" or "My favorite thing to do is _____" and have children dictate answers. We've found that "All About Me" books often become popular reading material for children, so be sure to laminate them for heavy use and then include them in your book nook. (For more ideas for the writing center, see chapter 8.)

Creating a chart like this with children can provide rich material for "All About Me" books.

Important Things to Know About Writing Development

When you think about all that happens as children develop into writers, you probably feel as we do—there is a lot going on! This section describes writing development based on both our experiences with young children and relevant research. Knowing this information will help you support your children's emergent literacy as you work with them in the writing center.

Writing Develops Over Time and Follows Common Stages

For decades, researchers have talked about levels of writing development (for example, Clay, 1975; Dyson, 1985; and Sulzby, 1985a). For example, Elizabeth Sulzby (1985a) collected and analyzed writing by children over their first few years of life. Here we describe her developmental continuum based on her research, which is made up of six levels of writing:

- writing through drawing
- writing through scribbling
- writing through letterlike forms
- writing by familiar units or letter strings
- writing through invented spelling
- writing through conventional spelling

These levels are not rigid and definite (Morrow, 1993). In other words, there is little to support the idea that children must progress through them in exactly the same way. Children may go back and forth between levels as they gain experience with writing, until writing through conventional spelling becomes comfortable to them. Children should have the option of writing at any level as they progress toward the final level.

Drawing and Writing: Ways of Communicating

Drawing and writing are both ways of representing. With drawing, we try to represent the object or idea directly, through pictures or images. With writing, we try to represent the object or idea indirectly, through symbols for the word for that object or idea. Of course, in both writing and drawing the representation may not be exact. For example, in drawing, a child may make a tree orange, or an abstract artist may make something that looks only vaguely like an actual tree. In writing, we may write "tree" when we actually mean a particular type of tree in a particular place.

That drawing and writing are both ways of representing is just one of many similarities between them, and it may be helpful to keep in mind that at the heart of each act is the intention to communicate an idea. Just as illustrators and writers both contribute to our comprehension of text, children communicate with us through drawing and writing. So when working with young children whose marks don't automatically signal whether their intention is to write or draw, it's important to ask children to tell you about what they have created.

It's important to recognize that drawing develops and is valuable in and of itself. Children's drawings convey important messages and serve as indicators of children's emerging abilities to create art (Kellogg, 1969). Victor Lowenfeld documented six stages of drawing development that occur in children between toddlerhood and adolescence (1954). The first two stages most likely apply to the children you teach:

Scribbling (ages 2 to 4 years)

Scribbling occurs with or without guidance from others and develops over time from disordered (uncontrolled) to longitudinal (controlled, repetitive) to circular (more complex, controlled) markings. (See figure 8.2.) As they near the end of this stage, children can usually name or tell stories about what they have drawn. However, they usually do not choose color with intention. They enjoy making large movements when they draw . . . and marks on surfaces such as walls (as you may know all too well!)

Preschematic (ages 4 to 7 years)

At this stage, children become more representational when they draw. For example, when drawing a human figure, they might use a circle for the head and vertical lines for the legs. (See figure 8.3.) They may not capture the space or relationship between objects or elements, but they are starting to capture the elements themselves from the world around them in their

FIGURE 8.2
A young child creates a work of art by scribbling.

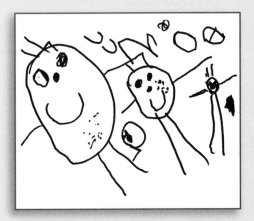

FIGURE 8.3
This child portrays the important people in her life—her parents and herself.

drawings. Cathy Malchiodi, director of the Institute for the Arts and Health, writes that Lowenfeld "emphasiz[es] the discovery of relationships among drawing, thinking, and reality" during this stage (1998, p. 83).

FIGURE 8.4
Writing through drawing.

Writing Through Drawing

Whether children are trying to capture their house, grandmother, pet, or any other subject for that matter, drawing pictures is one of the first ways they put their thoughts and ideas on paper (Baghban, 1984; Bissex, 1980). It is one of the first ways they tell stories. This makes sense because many early emergent readers believe that we read pictures in books, not words (Sulzby, 1985a, 1985b). See figure 8.4.

Writing Through Scribbling

Between the ages of 2 ½ and 3 years, many children begin to recognize differences between drawing and writing. Their drawing and writing may begin to look different. For example, their writing may be composed of squiggly lines but their drawing may be composed of circles and scribbles. See figure 8.5. Still, at these ages properties of drawing and writing are very much intermingled. When writing, children's marks may look writing-like but also represent some physical aspect of their topic. For example, children tend to create scribble-writing that represents the size of the object or person (Ferreiro & Teberosky, 1982). If the child's brother is older and taller than she, she may write his name in a string longer than her own name. Or if a child knows that a dog is bigger than a mouse, his scribbling of the word *mouse* may appear shorter or smaller than the string for *dog*.

Children also learn to structure their scribbling to resemble text structures they know. For example, in figure 1.1 on page 16, the first sample shows a little girl's scribbling of a grocery list. You can see how much the scribbles resemble an adult's typical shopping list.

FIGURE 8.5
Writing through scribbling.

Writing Through Letterlike Forms and Letter Strings

Following scribbling, young children begin to create letters and letterlike forms on paper to convey messages and ideas. Although these are not always conventionally formed letters, they look like letters. Children may write strings of letters that do not actually compose words, but which the children may refer to as words. Letters and shapes may also be included in the strings early on, though this will diminish as children increasingly come to see letters as a separate system. At this stage, children understand that writing is made up of something other than drawings and scribbles. It's made up of letters and words. This is an important milestone. See figure 8.6.

Writing Through Invented Spelling and Conventional Spelling

During the preschool years, children's letter formations become more conventional. Children also begin to match the sounds they hear to the letters that they write, and letters begin to represent syllables in words (Whitehurst & Lonigan, 2001). Representing sounds in words involves invented spelling (Neuman et al., 2000). Invented spelling is just that—children test out different ways words might be spelled, based on their knowledge of the sounds of letters and letter combinations. It's important to allow children to explore, try out, and play around with spellings in their own writing and in others' writing. See figure 8.7.

FIGURE 8.6
Writing through letterlike forms and letter strings.

FIGURE 8.7
Writing through invented spelling: "No one can come in except Mommy."

FIGURE 8.8
Writing through conventional spelling.

> **"** *. . . invented spelling not only allows children to write well before first grade, but it also builds essential literacy skills* (Neuman et al., 2000). **"**

Over time, children will gravitate toward more conventional spelling. That said, do not expect conventional spelling of most words from preschoolers, although don't be surprised if a few children demonstrate it. See figure 8.8.

Although we urge you to allow children to practice invented spelling, we also urge you to view it as a transition and not an endpoint. J. Richard Gentry (1978) has described five stages for first-grade spellers (summarized in Richgels, 2001, p. 147). Read them over and apply them to your children to determine where they are on the road to conventional spelling.

- precommunicative, which includes any writing attempts, such as letter strings and random letter formations, prior to invented spelling
- semiphonetic, which entails dependence on letter names, for example, writing *mt* for *empty*
- phonetic, in which there is an effort to represent vowel sounds in every syllable, such as *fet* for *feet*
- transitional, which includes awareness of and representations of other aspects of words, such as using two letters to represent a sound, for example, *chrie* for *try*
- correct stage, in which writers achieve conventional spelling

In addition to helping children move toward conventional spelling, invented spelling also helps children to gain phonemic awareness and an understanding of the alphabetic principle (the notion that words are made up of letters and that the letters stand for the sounds we make when we say the words and that by putting the letters together in various ways we make different words) (for example, Adams, 1990; Ehri, 1989). So invented spelling not only allows children to write well before first grade, but it also builds essential literacy skills (Neuman et al., 2000).

When children enter elementary school, they usually use a combination of invented spelling and conventional spelling in their writing. However, knowing these typical stages can help you to recognize where children are and where they are headed in their writing development. Having this knowledge allows you to appreciate all that children are doing to make meaning through writing.

Children's Drawings and Early Writing Mean Something

Regardless of their writing level, children have (and should be recognized as having) intentions for their writing. Acknowledging those intentions helps children understand why we write and that their attempts at writing mean something. For instance, a child may read you a string of letters he has written that he reports as saying, "the writing center has run out of paper," to remind you

To Correct or Not to Correct? The Answer May Surprise You

Do you ever wonder about whether to correct children's letter formations and invented spelling? Although it may seem counterintuitive, correcting may not facilitate writing development, and in some instances may hinder it. Young writers need to test boundaries—and when they do, they tend to make errors. It's important to view those errors not as problems, but as opportunities to learn about each writer (Clay, 1975). Common errors occur at each level of writing development; knowing these errors helps you place each child on the continuum. Correcting every error may discourage early

writers from fully exploring this new way of conveying meaning. When you allow developmentally appropriate errors, children become eager to write!

As early childhood educators, we should always be asking ourselves *why* we are considering making certain corrections and *how* those corrections will promote early writing skills. If you feel that particular children are not transitioning into the next level as you would expect, don't hesitate to intervene.

Perhaps one of your children always writes letter strings from right to left. You can model that we write from left to right a number of times in the day, such

as when you are writing names for jobs of the day in front of the whole group or when you're working with individual students as they write in their journals. Always ask children to write their name in the upper left corner of their paper (not the right, as students typically do in middle school). This orients children's eyes to the left and gives them nowhere else to go with their letters but to the right. Put a mark in the corner where they should start writing. See the section on page 153 entitled "Scaffolded Writing" for more ideas.

to stock up. This is a great opportunity to acknowledge that you understand the message. You can post it by the door to take on your way out to show children that what they write is meaningful to themselves and others.

A word of caution: If a child writes something that you can't read, ask him or her to read it to you rather than asking what it says. Asking what it says only reinforces the fact that their writing is illegible, which could have negative consequences.

Likewise, as we mentioned earlier, when children are drawing, we do not advocate asking them what their picture is because that implies that it has to "be" something. Perhaps a child just wants to draw "purple." If so, that's okay. Furthermore, by asking them what their picture is, we send the subtle message, "Whatever it's supposed to be, it doesn't look like that." Instead, try saying, "Tell me about it." You'll be amazed at the amount of information most children will give you.

Creating a Writing Center

One of the best ways to promote writing development in young children is to create and maintain a writing center (Morrow, 1990). The writing center is the central location for writing materials and exploration using those materials. This section includes a definition of the writing center, its benefits for writing development, guidelines for setting it up and stocking it, and, finally, some activities to do in the center.

What Is a Writing Center?

The writing center is a spot where children devote time and attention to writing. They might write in journals, create books, practice the alphabet and their names, compose messages to you and one another, create signs for use in other centers around the classroom. There are many possibilities. The writing center, like all centers, should entice children to investigate their world, particularly literacy in their world. For that to happen, it must contain the right materials, work surfaces, and display surfaces, all of which we will discuss shortly.

" One of the best ways to promote writing development in young children is to create and maintain a writing center (Morrow, 1990). "

The Benefits of a Writing Center to Writing Development

The writing center contains all the materials needed for children to engage with writing for concentrated periods of time. By making these materials available to children, and offering the right activities, we encourage children to enter the center and engage with writing. In the process, they will acquire motor skills needed to write and learn to write conventionally.

An effective writing center gives children ample exposure to the purposes for writing. It also encourages children to play with language and focus on language parts, which reading doesn't necessarily do (Clay, 1975). Specifically, the activities that children do in the writing center should help them

- realize there is a system and organization of print.

- begin to hear individual sounds in words, which indicates they're developing phonemic awareness. (See chapter 2.)

An effective writing center includes a multitude of writing tools, ample space to write, and plenty of opportunities to write. Displays of print provide useful models for emergent writers.

- begin to match letters to the sounds they hear, which indicates whether they're developing letter-sound knowledge. (See chapter 2.)

- practice decoding letters and sounds in the messages they have written. It's easier for some children to read their own writing than somebody else's at the same level.

The following section discusses how to create and stock a writing center that will help children develop not only writing skills but also an interest in writing.

Stocking the Writing Center

Teachers often ask us for ideas for making writing centers appealing, so here we offer a few. Most of them work best with children 2½ and older, but toddlers may enjoy and be able to handle some of them as well.

- A typewriter. (In this age of computers, be prepared to explain what it is!)

- A variety of writing materials such as colored pencils, pencils that look like sticks, markers, crayons, ballpoint pens, gel pens, rubber stamps and ink pads, thin markers,

Setting Up the Writing Center

If your classroom does not have a writing center, you may be wondering where to even begin. Here are some ideas to get the writing center up and running:

- Create mailboxes for each child, labeled with pictures and names of the children. Children can correspond with one another by writing messages and placing them in these mailboxes. They'll look forward to receiving mail from a friend!

- Provide child-size furnishings such as desks, tables, and chairs. It's important for children to be comfortable as they engage in writing experiences, such as writing letters, journal entries, and original stories.

- Make sure materials are organized, visible, and accessible for children.

- Create space for displaying children's stories, poems, news, notes, and announcements on a bulletin board or directly on the wall.

(Morrow, 2002)

Once you've set up the writing center think about stocking it. From there, ideas for making the most of it will flow!

special papers, tape, a stapler, child-safe scissors, and anything else you believe will spur writing. Rotate materials so something new appears each week.

- A box of magazine photos to use as story starters. Encourage children to bring pictures from home and include a request for pictures in your newsletter.

- A file box with each child's name and photo on a card. This can serve as an address box so children can write notes to each other.

Tools for writing can include classics like chalk and chalkboards and dry-erase boards and markers, or trendier tools such as gel pens, gel boards, and different-shaped pencils.

- Envelopes from card shops. (When customers buy cards, they often forget to take an envelope. As a result, card shops routinely have extras.)

- A writing box for each child made out of a box containing paper, writing utensils, literacy-related odds and ends (for example, used postage stamps, stickers, rubber stamps), an alphabet list, a word book (to record words the child likes to use), and a "research journal" (to record ideas and collect information for projects). Children can personalize their boxes by writing their names on them and decorating them.

- Nonpaper writing tools such as magnet doodle boards, dry-erase boards, chalkboards, and gel boards.

- An alphabet frieze and picture dictionaries such as *My First Word Book* (Wilkes, 1997).

- Charts created during whole-group activities, such as "words related to_____ [a theme]" and "what I like to do with my family." Encourage children to use words from these charts in their writing.

If you practice scaffolded writing on a regular basis, children will gradually move to writing more independently. They can plan what they want to say, create lines, and write on their own the message that they have practiced with you or a new message. Sources such as a common-word chart, a word wall, and an alphabet frieze help them accomplish their writing tasks. Research shows that kindergartners who engaged in scaffolded writing, even children considered "at risk," produced greater amounts of work than children who didn't, and they often chose to engage in writing activities even after the designated writing time ended (Bodrova & Leong, 1998).

Journal Writing

Journal writing gives children a way to think about written language and to experiment with writing their thoughts on paper. It also gives you an authentic purpose for talking about how thinking and writing are connected, since the reason for keeping a journal is to capture thoughts in writing. Here are some ways to introduce journals and help young children use them:

Explain How and Why to Use a Journal. Explain to children the basic purposes and procedures for keeping a journal. For instance, you can say that when you have something on your mind, you like to write it down in your journal, which helps you to remember or work through an issue. You might say that you had such a wonderful picnic over the weekend that you wrote and drew about it in your journal. Or you might say that when you are feeling sad, you like to write about happy things to make you feel better. You can show them that journal writing allows you to collect ideas over time and that you can always revisit what you have written and remember each occasion again. Finally, you can demonstrate some basic conventions of journal writing, such as dating every entry. We don't expect that children will date each entry but supplying a date stamp for them at the writing center may encourage them to think about it.

Photo: Shenglan Zhang

This teacher scaffolds a young writer by providing a model of a word and guiding the student as she attempts to write that word herself.

Accept Writing at All Levels. As children gain control over their writing, journal entries may contain drawing, scribbling, invented spelling, or conventional spelling. All forms should be welcomed, encouraged, and supported. As children think about what to put in their journals, they should be focusing on getting the thoughts in their heads onto the page—not necessarily on conventional use of language.

Use Journal Time to Scaffold Emergent Writing. Journal-writing time can be the perfect time to guide a child who is struggling to get a message down in words. (See previous section on scaffolded writing for information on how to help that child.)

Use Journals for Informal Assessment. If you want to monitor emergent writers' development throughout the year, keep an eye on them during journal time (Soderman, Gregory, & O'Neill, 1999). Whether journal time is an activity area available every day, or just some days, take time to check in with and make notes on individual children as they make entries. Then compare notes periodically. By doing so, you can see how their writing is progressing and give support as needed.

Use Journals As a Reference. When children have a question about writing—for example, when they want to remember how they wrote or drew something—they often find it helpful to refer back to their journals to see how they've handled the question in the past. Journals can serve as a resource for children, so encourage them to consult entries whenever there's a need.

Photo: Alison Billman

Journaling allows emergent writers the freedom and space to explore writing on their own terms, an important step toward conventional writing.

Many Activities, One Location

Additional activities for the writing center include

Here, three children compose messages with help from one another, using an old typewriter in the writing center.

Photo: Pamela Green

- generating a poster for the new theme in dramatic play, labels for the newest additions to a garden, traffic signs for roadways constructed in the block area, or any other kind of print for use in other centers.

- corresponding with friends through mailboxes in your writing center—and writing letters to family members and friends.

- writing a story or fact book, and creating a tape recording of it for others to hear. You can package the child-written books and tapes to send home to parents.

- sharing children's writing. After doing this, don't be surprised if you have a run on the writing center, since one child's work can inspire others when it comes to finding new purposes or new topics for writing. When children share their work, they see firsthand that the purpose of writing is to communicate ideas, and they also get a reaction to their writing.

At Nora Thompson's early childhood center, the writing center is well stocked and used for authentic writing activities. For example, after ladybugs were spotted crawling all around the building (during the spring, Michigan is often inundated with ladybugs), Nora suggested that if the children created a more preferable home for the bugs, they might be able to stop the invasion. So the children decided to make a ladybug farm. The children put a great deal of thought into accessories that the ladybugs would appreciate, such as a water slide. Print was also included. One child even thought to write an exit sign so that ladybugs would know how to leave when they were finished enjoying the farm.

Children wrote—using scribbles, letter strings, or invented spelling— directions to the ladybug farm to help their "guests" find it. They also wrote notes to the bugs, expressing their feelings about their bothersome behavior and how they would like the bugs to vacate the building and go to the ladybug farm. This idea started with Nora talking with the children and ended with them writing directions, notes, signs, and so much more. Activities like this one can make writing in your writing center meaningful and enjoyable for children.

Here is the exit sign that Nora Thompson's young writers created, which was used in a "lady bug farm" to direct occupants to the way out.

Concluding Thoughts

There is a lot to know about young children's writing development. But gaining that knowledge is worth the effort because it can help you plan and put into practice developmentally appropriate instruction and activities. Although writing should have a place in every corner of your classroom, the writing center is a central place where children can access materials to write and engage with written language. With your help, children will learn that they can communicate ideas and emotions to others through writing, and that writing is not only an important skill, but an enjoyable one.

- all kinds of texts—especially informational texts—to serve as resources for learning about the natural world.

- posters, graphs, diagrams, and other print resources that describe and show aspects of the world.

Sciencing Around

Sally Kilmer and Helenmarie Hofman refer to "hands-on, brains-on" active involvement in science as "sciencing" (1995, p. 44). Sciencing can happen informally—for example, when a child suddenly wonders what makes her light-up sneakers light up—or formally, as part of an organized class project on the water cycle, for example. Activities can begin outside or at home and be brought into the science center (Worth & Grollman, 2003). For instance, during outdoor play, a child may find an interesting plant and, at science-center time, may go about answering questions such as "What is this plant?" "How does it grow?" and "Where does it usually live?" With the help of some

"Sciencing around" happens best with the right equipment. At this center, children investigate insects using books, containers, plastic figures, and their own observation skills.

of the materials listed on pages 175–176, children can make observations and document their questions and discoveries in their journals—in whatever form they are most comfortable. Having bugs roaming around the classroom may seem like a pesky problem, but it can also be the source of wonder for young children—and an opportunity for sciencing, too. These are just two examples of interesting things to investigate at the science center.

Preschoolers and older children can also take on the role of scientist and make hypotheses about whether certain objects, such as a rock, a toy tugboat, a toy car, and a plastic cup, will sink or float in a tub of water. They can record their observations and write down why they think some objects sink and some don't. You can also bring in some research journals from real scientists to show how literacy plays a leading role for them. Try to find articles that relate to investigations going on in the science center and share them with the children to help them make connections between their own observations and hypotheses and those of real scientists.

The Sensory Table: Texture *and* Literacy Learning

Little fingers exploring sand, water, textured letters, and other materials should be common in early childhood settings. The sensory table, or the texture table, as it's sometimes called, can provide all the right materials for children to explore using all five senses.

The sensory table can be filled with many different materials that not only feel interesting but also promote literacy. Rotating materials gives children the opportunity to explore many different types of textures. Talking about what they are feeling, seeing, and perhaps smelling can enrich their vocabularies as well. Consider:

Sand By placing sand in the sensory table, children can practice forming letters and words with their fingers, which doesn't require the fine motor skills that using a pencil does. Encourage

The texture table can be filled with a variety of materials that invite little hands.

them by asking them to write their names (or the first letter in their names) and other favorite words.

Seashells Place seashells in the sand table and have children search for them and then sort them by type with the help of books on shells and pictures of different kinds of shells. From there, make a chart of the seashells that they find and display it nearby.

Leaves During outdoor play in the fall, have children collect vibrant leaves and place them in brown paper bags as part of a nature treasure hunt. Later, place leaves and other natural objects (such as pinecones and pine needles) in the sensory table. Have children sort leaves and other objects by color, shape, and size. Children's books such as *Autumn Leaves* by Ken Robbins (2003) can be useful in determining the origin of the leaves and other objects.

Other Possible Materials for the Sensory Table:

- snow
- water
- birdseed (be careful of nut allergies)
- cracked corn and corn on the cob
- wrapping or scrap paper and child-safe scissors
- playing cards
- cotton balls and tongs
- packing peanuts
- "treasure," such as coins and glass stones

(With these and all materials discussed, be sure to consider the age of the children you are working with. Some of these objects are choking hazards for children under 3, others are fine for infants and up.)

You can also use texture books to enhance your sensory table. A classic example is *Pat the Bunny* by Dorothy Kunhardt (1940), but now bookstores are stocked with many other choices, including *Touch and Feel: Farm* (1998), *Touch and Feel: Shapes* (2000), *Touch and Feel: Clothes* (1998), and many more board books from Dorling Kindersley Publishing, as well as Barney Saltzberg's "kisses" books: *Animal Kisses* (2000), *Baby Animal Kisses* (2001), *Peekaboo Kisses* (2002), and *Noisy Kisses* (2004), which contain synthetic animal fur and feathers and are available through Red Wagon Books. Other touch-and-feel books include materials such as tire rubber and shiny foil. As very young children explore these books with their hands, you can introduce them to textures and print.

Concluding Thoughts

Every center in your room can give children opportunities to engage with print through a variety of materials and activities. Literacy can extend beyond the writing center and the book nook, and into centers devoted to art, block building, computers, listening, manipulatives, puppet play, science, and textures. The more frequently children find themselves in situations that require literacy, the more likely they will be to understand its power and use it in their lives.

Photo: Raymond Coutu

Painting outdoors provides wonderful opportunities for children to explore literacy on a grand scale.

Live Large... and Messy

Again, it's important to do all we can to encourage writing and drawing, in fresh, engaging ways. But, let's face it, some projects are just too big and/or disorderly for the classroom. By clothespinning butcher paper or rolled art paper to a fence, you create a large, appealing canvas for writing and drawing. Paper can also be cut to the actual size and shape of everyday items such as street signs, animals, and household appliances. Given their scale, activities like these are much easier to manage outdoors.

Outdoors may also be a better place for messy, hands-on writing and drawing activities such as finger painting, using spray foam, and creating works from sand. Activities like these are not only great fun but provide great practice in letter formation and other forms of mark making. Children literally *feel* the writing.

Offer Books Related to What Children See Outdoors

Making connections between real life and texts is important to understanding and learning from text and to using reading and writing in our lives. Good readers routinely do it (Duke & Pearson, 2002). So we should encourage young children to do it, too. For example, if children encounter insects outdoors, you might help them use the book *Insects and Crawly Creatures* (Royston, 1992) to identify those insects. You might also carry out the Experience-Text-Relationship activity based on *Insects and Crawly Creatures*, described in chapter 4, page 86. For additional ideas, see the box entitled "Eight Great Books for the Great Outdoors."

Sing and Move

As discussed in chapter 5, songs and rhymes can be powerful tools for developing phonological awareness. Outdoors is a great place to sing songs that invite a lot of movement, such as this:

I'm running, running, running, I'm running,
running, running, I'm running, running, running,
and now I stop!

I'm tippytoeing, tippytoeing, tippytoeing, I'm
tippytoeing, tippytoeing, tippytoeing, I'm tippytoeing,
tippytoeing, tippytoeing, and now I stop!

(and so on)

Children also enjoy forming letters with their bodies, individually or in groups, to songs such as "YMCA." William Wegman's *ABC* (1994) depicts dogs amusingly positioned to form alphabet letters. Read it before going outside to have children create letters using their own bodies.

Encourage Jump-Rope Rhymes

The rhymes used in jump-rope play can promote phonological awareness and concept of word, which is the understanding that speech is divided into words, with words separated by spaces when they are written. You can write out the words to these rhymes just as you might for songs you sing inside. Then laminate them for durability, if you wish, and post them near the jump-rope site. Extend learning by allowing children to use Say, Say, Oh Playmate, a software program that builds on children's knowledge of jump-rope rhymes (Pinkard, 2000), or reading aloud rhymes that come in book form, such as *Miss Mary Mack* (Hoberman, 1998).

Eight Great Books for the Great Outdoors

Infants

- *Baby Outside* by Neil Ricklem. Little Simon, 1991

- *Water Play* by Margaret Miller. Simon & Schuster, 1997

Toddlers

- *About Birds: A Guide for Children* by Cathryn Sill, illustrated by John Sill. Peachtree, 1991

- *The Big Book of Things That Go.* Dorling Kindersley, 1994 (for the pictures, not so much for the text)

- *We're Going on a Bear Hunt* by Michael Rosen. Illustrated by Helen Oxenbury. Margaret K. McElderry Books, 1989

Preschoolers

- *Insects and Crawly Creatures* by Angela Royston. Photographs by Jerry Young. Little Simon, 1992

- *In the Woods: Who's Been Here?* by Lindsay Barrett George. Greenwillow Books, 1995

- *Nature Spy* by Shelley Rotner and Ken Kreisler. Photographs by Shelley Rotner. Scholastic, 1992

A trip to an ice cream parlor presents opportunities to read flavor tags and many other texts.

Consider a field trip to an ice cream parlor.

- *Before* the trip, you could read aloud a book about how ice cream is made (such as *Let's Find Out About Ice Cream* by Mary Ebeltoft Reid, 1996). You could show where the ice cream parlor is located on a map and read the parlor's menu or list of ice cream flavors.

- *During* the field trip, you could focus on the labels of ice cream flavors. Read the flavors to children, but also allow them to figure them out using clues from the words (if they have some letter knowledge) and the context (the appearance of the ice cream). Other print—the cone display, the store hours, the signs on bathroom doors—will undoubtedly be worth pointing out as well.

- *After* the trip, you and the children could graph ice cream flavors according to preference. (Many parlors will provide an ice cream tasting as well as individual cones for children so that they can sample options before they commit to one.) You could write a thank-you note to the parlor's staff. You could write a book or poster with children, telling the story of the trip. (Be sure to take photographs during the trip if you plan to do this.) Put the book on display for parents or children and teachers in another class to read. You could also make ice cream together by following a recipe that you put on chart paper. A dramatic play area with props from the ice cream parlor (menus, order pads, recipe cards, and so forth) allows children to re-create and extend the experience into their play.

We went to the market on April 9th.

We saw lots of different kinds of vegetables.

1   2

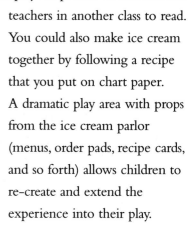

A class writes a book about its field trip to a local market.

Four Literacy-Focused Field-Trip Destinations to Consider

The library, bookstore, local newspaper headquarters, and post office are natural destinations for literacy-focused field trips. Here are some tips for making the most of your visits to them:

Library

Most libraries have programs for young children—and if they don't, most librarians are happy to organize an event for them. For example, your librarian might read aloud to the children and then lead an art project related to the book. Be sure to call ahead to arrange the visit. If you are working on a topic or theme, let the librarian know. She may be willing to gather related books in advance. Also, be sure to let the librarian know the age range of the children you are bringing so that she can choose books and arrange the space appropriately. For example, a library near us has a "Library Babies" program for infants, which looks very different from the preschool program it offers.

When children arrive, let them explore the library before they settle down for the Read Aloud to minimize the chances of them becoming antsy during the Read Aloud. Allow each child to select one book for you to check out. Or, if you're not comfortable with that, allow each child to share a book briefly show-and-tell style so that children become familiar with the range of books available to them. Plan to return to the library as often as you can. If you are located far from a library, visits may happen only once a season or even just once a year. But if you're close, go every week!

Bookstore

Most bookstores have a special children's book buyer who is more knowledgeable about literature for young people and literacy instruction than other staffers. If you call ahead, the buyer may plan a Read Aloud and/or put together a set of books on a theme or topic you are studying. He may also arrange a special activity with the children such as a book-inspired snack or art project. As with the library, it often makes sense to allow children to explore first and then settle in for a Read Aloud. Because children cannot "check out" books but may see books

> **Dear**
>
> _____,
> [The name that the child uses for the parent(s) or guardian(s)]
>
> **Today we went to the bookstore. I really liked the book** _____
> [book title]
> **by** _____.
> [book author]
>
> **Love,**
>
> _____
> [The child's name]

because they are treated like readers. When you casually ask, "Did you read the clean-up sign?" to the child who doesn't seem to be following it, the underlying assumption is not that he isn't cleaning up because he doesn't want to, but rather because he didn't get a chance to read the sign. Of course, if he had read the sign he would be cleaning up!

This strategy also encourages children to start using the vocabulary of reading. For example, the child walking around with the sign might say, "Did you read the sign?" to the child who is ignoring her. Children will complain, "I didn't get to read the sign!" Reading text becomes expected and valuable.

Using Text for Management Beyond Transitions

Monitoring the safety of many small, sometimes uncooperative, bodies at once is one of our greatest challenges as early childhood educators. We must set limits to manage traffic flow, to encourage appropriate use of materials, and to keep an eye on every child in the room. Usually, we convey these limits orally, but we also put them in writing to accomplish several things:

- to promote children's interaction with text

- to model another use of text

- to encourage children to use text independently to figure out what to do

- to add to our environmental print

Make signs for each activity area announcing how many children are allowed to play there, showing a numeral, the word for the numeral, and some sort

Through numerals and symbols, a sign in this classroom's block area shows that up to four children are allowed to play there.

of graphic representation of the numeral, for example, the word *three*, the numeral *3*, and three stick figures. Over time, children make connections between and among words and symbols. This notion of representation is critical as children learn to associate letters and the sounds they stand for. Toddlers who cannot yet accurately count the number of children in the activity area themselves can still benefit from hearing you read the sign and count the number of children in an area to determine whether there is room for them.

Children can create signs for areas and activities. This child, for example, created a sign for a block structure that says, "Please do not move."

Promote health, safety, and a tidy environment with other signs containing combinations of text and symbols. You could post an octagonal sign on your door that says, "Stop! Only grown-ups open this door!" As you read the sign to the children, they will not only associate the shape of the sign with the message, but they'll learn an important lesson about how messages are conveyed. Other signs you might include are

- Wash Your Hands, posted over the sink,

- Flush, near the toilet,

- Park Trucks Here, in the block area,

- One Way, at the top of the slide or on a bike path,

- Throw Trash Here, on the garbage can.

These signs are most effective when you add a symbol to help children figure out the text's message. For example, for the Park Trucks Here sign, you might show five toy trucks lined next to one another, with lines separating them. You should also read the signs to children periodically to remind them of what they say and why.

More About Cooking and Literacy

There are many ways to weave literacy into cooking experiences. As we've said, children can read the recipe, but they can also read the labels on ingredients and document their favorite recipes from home. They can retell what they did first, what they did next, and so on to help you chart the sequence of events in creating a dish. They can reenact real cooking experiences in the dramatic play area, using make-believe ingredients, following procedures like mixing, stirring, and baking, and sharing the appropriate vocabulary. Cooking is one of those high-interest activities that can lure almost any child to check out what is going on. Using that interest to promote literacy skills is smart. To ensure a cooking activity's success, be sure to

- select a recipe with few ingredients.

- select a recipe with few steps.

- select a recipe for something that the kids will be interested in eating (such as blueberry muffins) or using (such as play dough).

- chart the recipe out so children can see the steps (and for later reference). Remember the first step is always "Wash your hands!"

- invite children to carry out each step in small groups. One group mixes the dry ingredients, for example, one group mixes the wet ingredients, one group mixes the two together, another group scoops the muffins into cups for baking, etc.

- discourage children from licking utensils and fingers.

- plan to eat or use the recipe that day for maximum impact.

- allow children to get excited by the process. It's a real treat to be able to do a "grown-up" task like cooking! Use a quiet, steady tone if things begin to get out of hand.

One teacher we know created a "cookbook" by clipping all of her charted recipes to a clothes hanger. When she wants to use a recipe with children, she just pulls it out from the stack, moves it to the front, and then hangs the whole "cookbook" near her food-prep area. By doing this, she can focus on promoting language and literacy rather than worry about preparing for and setting up the task.

This well-organized cooking center allows children to see the names of ingredients and then match them to recipes they create with the teacher.

Each step should have an accompanying symbol to help children who cannot yet read text. When working with children, casually check to see if they're using the chart. For example, ask them if they washed their hands. If they don't have a napkin, ask them to read the chart to see what they should do. You may be surprised at how quickly children start to monitor themselves. And you may be delighted by how they are beginning to use text for guidance.

These children enjoy a snack by moving from station to station and following these directions:

1. wash hands.

2. Put 1 scoop of raisins in cup.

3. Put 1 scoop of crackers in cup.

4. Put 1 scoop of chocolate chips in cup.

5. Mix.

6. Enjoy!

Diapering and Other Bathroom-Related Delights

Perhaps the most unlikely time to find opportunities to build children's literacy is while you're diapering them or toilet training them, or while they're using the facilities on their own. It can be done, though. Here's how:

Diapering

Many teachers hate this part of the job. Susan, on the other hand, loves it because it offers quiet, one-on-one time with children in an otherwise busy day. As she cleans, diapers, and dresses children individually, she listens to what they say and takes note of what

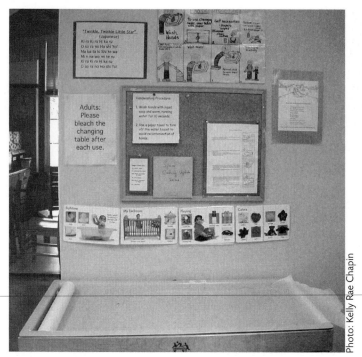

This diapering area is enhanced by a "wall book" for children to enjoy, as well as procedural texts for adults to follow. There is also a song posted for teachers to sing while changing children.

Photo: Kelly Rae Chapin

they are observing. To build oral language, she posts pictures associated with her theme near the changing table. As she and the child look at and talk about the pictures, she reinforces concepts that were introduced at group time. For example, if your theme is "pets," you might post pictures of dogs, cats, fish, guinea pigs, or other animals that fit the theme. Posting songs or poems near the table also gives her material to promote children's language development.

Allow toddlers to look at books while you change them. If you have a mirror near your changing table, have toddlers look at their reflections as you talk about and show them pages from books such as *Baby Talk* by Margaret Miller (2004). This helps her make text-to-self connections, which is important to comprehension, as discussed in chapter 4.

Bathrooming

Bathrooming is a significant and necessary part of each child's day, especially if he or she is in the process of being toilet trained or has recently been toilet trained. Making reading materials available in the bathroom ensures that children are interacting with text.

Providing a book basket or wall-mounted book rack in the bathroom offers easy access to reading materials that, perhaps, match whatever theme you're exploring in the classroom.

Because it's important to always maintain sanitary conditions in our settings, we encourage you to use vinyl bath books or books with laminated pages, which are easy to clean. You can also create "wall books" by disassembling regular books, laminating the pages, and posting them on the wall. Wall books are effective anywhere, but inside a bathroom stall is an especially good place for them, given the captive audience. We have all had children who sit and sit and sit in the bathroom. Giving them something to read can make the time a little more valuable.

Also, consider posting procedures, like those mentioned earlier for the eating area, in your bathroom. Refer to the text when you talk with children by saying, "I'm wondering if you flushed" and pointing to the symbol and text that says "Flush." Or saying, "Did you wash your hands?" and pointing to the symbol of the hands under running water and the text that says "Wash your hands." You can also point out to children that grown-ups read certain signs to help them remember what to do, such as diapering-procedure charts and cleaning schedules. All of these experiences show children that text is all around them and used for many purposes.

Photo: Kelly Rae Chapin

Young children spend a lot of time in toileting areas. So enrich those spaces by posting thematically related texts.

Concluding Thoughts

When it comes to the custodial aspects of working with young children, we often feel too rushed or overwhelmed to advance their learning. But we should try our best. Consider looking at each contact that you have with a child as an opportunity to develop his or her literacy skills and understandings. Whether you are feeding children, transitioning them, or diapering them, you are in a literacy-learning moment. Don't waste it!

Spalding Times

Newsletter
March 21, 2005
AM

Head Teacher: Grace Spaulding
Student Teachers: Michelle Conley
Annie Nepiuk
Andrea Yocum

Greetings!
Over the past week, the theme was insects. The children learned what characteristics determine whether or not a creature is an insect. They also took on the role of entomologists and visitors at the insect house in pretend play. The children observed the insects and recorded their findings. Together, the children created a class caterpillar, an insect collage, and built insect habitats. During large group, they learned the life cycle of a butterfly and acted out the stages. The children enjoyed singing familiar songs and learning new ones such as, "Twinkle, twinkle firefly," and "Head, thorax, abdomen" (to the tune of "Head, shoul...

Since the music makers unit, many children hav... exploring the pretend spiders in our class. Bec... is now the theme. The children will learn what... insects, how they create their webs, and the m... spiders. In pretend play, the children will obse... pretend spiders, collect data, and take on the r... addition, the children will work together to mai... webs and create a class quilt of spider drawing...

To extend your child's experience with spiders... a spider hunt inside and outside your house. As... characteristics are that make a creature a spid... on the spiders you find. Search around for spi... child to describe the similarities and differenc... found. You could also sing a song about spiders... might already be familiar with is, "The Itsy Bit...

Reminder: Field Trip to the MSU Bughouse on...
9:30 - 1...

Spiders: Terms, Facts, and Principles

1. Spiders are arachnids, not insects.
2. Spiders have two main body parts: the cephalothorax (head and thorax combined) and the abdomen.
3. Spiders have eight legs and eight eyes.
4. Spiders cannot see well at all.
5. Spiders have fangs at the tip of each jaw and pedipalps alongside each jaw. The fangs contain a poison that is strong enough to kill insects; the pedipalps assist in feeling and also aid in holding prey.
6. Spiders have silk producing spinnerets, which is how they make spider webs.
7. Spiders have a hard outer body covering with joints in the legs so they can bend.
8. Most of the spider's senses are in its legs.
9. Spiders feed on insects, worms, and their own kind. Some even eat fish, lizards, or birds.
10. Most spiders produce silk and weave webs. Those are called web spiders (ex: house or garden spiders).
11. Spiders use silk to make nests, cocoons, or webs for trapping insects.

Weekly Overview

Theme: Spiders
Date: March 21-24
Head Teacher: Spalding AM
Lead Student Teacher: Michelle Conley

Domain	Monday	Tuesday	Wednesday	Thursday	Back Up
Aesthetics	Spider webbing in sensory table	Pie tin spider web with marbles and white paint	Shaving cream and spiders in sensory table	Explore the MSU Bughouse	Spider web rubbings
Affective	Miss Spider computer game	Care for live spiders	Make a thumbprint spider	Hold live spiders and insects appropriately	
Cognitive	Count spider legs	Connect the dot spider web	Sort spiders/not spiders	Classify insects and spiders at the MSU Bughouse	Count spider eyes
Construction	Create spider hats	Construct spiders with Styrofoam balls	Create spiders with chocolate frosting and pretzels	Construct spider webs with yarn	Construct spider environments with spider webbing
Language	Sing "Spider Spinning"	Record spider observations	Spider rhymes	Discuss observations at the bughouse	Sing "Itsy Bitsy Spider"
Physical	Draw a spider	Gym: paddles and balls, tunnels, bowling, parachute	Dance with Mary Jane	Spider crawl	Sew spider webs
Pretend Play	Science lab:	Observe live spiders	Collect data	Be arachnologists	
Social	Create a class quilt of spider drawings	Take turns using spiders in water table	Make a class book: Spider Webs	Invite a friend to observe spiders/insects	Work together to create spider habitats
Large Group Focus	Introductions to spiders: similarities and differences compared to insects	Read The Itsy Bitsy Spider	Read Spiders and Their Webs	Field trip expectations and discussion	
Participating Parents Arrive at 8:10 am	3/21 Tom Welch 3/28 Doug Miller	3/22 Cheryl Miller 3/29 Sortman/Carr	3/23 Bres 3/30 Nicole Pasikowski	3/24 Jen Rule 3/31 Roberts	

MSU is an Affirmative Action/Equal Opportunity Institution

In the News: Newsletters That People Actually Read

Many teachers send home weekly or monthly newsletters featuring accomplishments, requests, and upcoming events. Consider adding quotations from children as that will create interest—parents and children will want to see what they and their friends had to say in the newsletter. Writing that results from language experience activities lends itself well to newsletters. For example, you might ask children the question "What happens in the winter?" and print their responses in the newsletter. Families will see the range of answers and extend the conversation at home.

Similarly, sending home information about things you discuss and do at school can

When Languages Collide: Supporting Home Languages

When we have children whose first language is not the language we use at school, we must make every effort to honor that language. Research tells us that developing a strong first language actually facilitates later literacy learning in English (Burns, Griffin, & Snow, 1999). Sending home newsletters and other materials in the child's home language is wise. If you don't have an interpreter on staff, tap a bilingual parent to assist you. Nearby colleges may also have people who could help. Always have a native speaker read over what you plan to send out, though. One administrator we know sent out a recruiting flyer that said the program kept children "in large cages"! Needless to say, enrollments were down that year.

also prompt healthy interactions between parents and children. Here's an example of what you might print:

> We visited the ice cream parlor today. The children were taken behind the scenes to see how ice cream is made. We watched each step in the process and then had a chance to taste a completed batch. Ask your child what part he or she liked the best and what flavor ice cream we got to taste. See if he or she wants to go back!

Tuesday

We went to the library this morning to check out pond books and played on their computers. We enjoyed outside time.
This afternoon we made thank-you cards for Holly, our tour guide from Woldumar. We introduced a new word to the word wall. The list is getting pretty long! The children have been focusing on sounding out and writing.

Posting news on charts, bulletin boards, or chalkboards outside the classroom is a great way to supplement a weekly newsletter.

You might follow this section with a description of how you extended learning back in the classroom—perhaps you made a batch of ice cream and read a book about ice cream. From there, you could include the recipe so the family can re-create the experience at home. You might also include the results of a survey on children's favorite ice cream flavors. In short, keep parents in the loop so they can support what's happening in your program.

Finally, newsletters are a great place to make our practices transparent to families. Tell parents not only *what* you are doing but also *why* you are doing it. For example, tell them you took dictation from children about the ice cream parlor experience to help them start to see that words can be captured and saved through writing, or you modeled a form of letter writing by writing a thank-you note to the ice cream parlor staff. Help parents to see your literacy goals for their children.

Parents are our partners. As such, we must communicate as we would with any collaborator. Keep them apprised of your thinking and your work and actively seek their feedback, suggestions, and support. Together, you can wrap children in literacy during every waking hour.

Concluding Thoughts

Though our relationships with children are powerful, they are also fleeting. Their parents' influence will go on long after we are out of the picture. One of the best ways to ensure our children's ongoing literacy development is to educate their families about literacy. By employing a variety of strategies, we can help parents see how important they are in their children's literacy lives.

Frequently Asked Questions

Over the years, at countless presentations and consultations, teachers of young children have asked us many questions about the best ways to build literacy into early childhood education. In this section, we answer the questions we get most often. If you have a question that we don't answer here, contact us at the Michigan State University's Child Development Laboratories, 325 W. Grand River, East Lansing, MI 48823.

Q How do I convince my administrator to allow me to include more literacy experiences in my program? She thinks they're developmentally inappropriate for young children.

A She's not alone. Many, many people think that we are cramming literacy down young children's tender throats. Why don't we agree? Because your administrator and others like her seem to hold the traditional view that literacy development is based on a "readiness model." That is, children have to reach a certain age or stage before they are ready to learn about literacy. We now know that children are gaining literacy understandings from the first time they hear a human voice. Your administrator probably also doesn't realize that the definition of literacy embraces not only conventional reading but also writing, listening, speaking, and viewing.

If you plan to provide phonics worksheets or flash cards to toddlers, your administrator is right: That is inappropriate. However, our guess is that you're not planning to do that, and the real issue is that your administrator doesn't understand that literacy develops long before elementary school begins, encompassing vocabulary learning, playing with words, scribble-writing, and much more.

Have a conversation with your administrator about what you've learned. Share this book with her. Broadening her view of literacy may be the key. Once she gets that, we suspect, she will support your efforts.

Q I have a parent who wants me to give worksheets to her child so that he'll be ready for kindergarten. I don't think I should do that. What can I say to her?

A Every parent wants his or her child to be successful. Congratulations on having one that is actively involved in her child's learning. That said, sometimes we teachers disagree with the methods parents advocate. We have found that the most productive way to deal with conflicting ideas is to sit down with the parent for a few minutes. Not a phone conversation, not a brief talk at drop-off or pickup time, rather, a conference. When you meet, ask the parent what she is doing at home to promote her child's literacy success. Then, let her know what you are doing at school to promote that success. Be specific. Help her understand, for example, that reading to children familiarizes them with concepts of print, that signing in each day allows them to practice writing their names and recognizing letters, that using empty labeled containers in the dramatic play area encourages children to practice reading familiar words in their environment. Let her know that these activities are likely to be more helpful and appropriate for her child's age than worksheets. Help her to see all the good work that you are doing, how it's contributing to her child's understanding of literacy concepts, and how it's setting the stage for formal instruction in reading and writing in elementary school.

Chances are, when one parent asks a question, others have the same question but are not asking it. So consider dedicating a regular section of your weekly or monthly newsletter to explaining an aspect of your literacy program. Invite parents to come in and see what you do. Make them your partners in promoting literacy. Don't be surprised if in time they move from being your partners to being your advocates.

Q Our program doesn't have a large budget for curriculum materials. How can we enrich our literacy environment with very limited funds?

A If it's any consolation, this is a question that most early childhood educators ask themselves every day. The easiest solution, of course, is to increase tuition to cover the cost of curriculum materials. But is that something we really want to do to young families that are already financially stressed? Our challenge, then, is providing great environments that meet the needs and challenge the minds of our young charges at the best value possible. In chapter 7, we offer several ideas. Having done this for a while, we have a few more tricks to share.

- **Know thy neighborhood businesses.** Local businesses such as stationery stores, bookstores, newsstands, art and photo supply stores, and office-services shops may have supplies to offer that might otherwise be thrown away. For example, Susan once received an entire box of textured fuchsia paper from a print shop because the box it had been delivered in was smashed and the paper was too crimped for the shop to use. The 3-year-olds loved it.

- **Put the word out.** When you have a need for something, tell as many people as you

can about it. For example, when we started a lending library for a toddler program recently, we asked families at the elementary and middle schools for gently used board books that they no longer needed. We received so many books, we barely had enough storage space!

- **Tap government agencies, national groups, and the Internet.** If you want teaching materials, especially posters, on nearly any topic you can get them for free from some government agency. Good agencies to try include the U.S. Department of Agriculture for anything to do with food (http://www.usda.gov), and the Michigan Department of Natural Resources (http://www.Michigan.gov/dnr) for anything to do with animals, water cycles,

or forestry. The National Wildlife Federation has materials as well. Try them at http://www.nwf.org. All of these Web sites have sections just for kids that you may find useful.

- **Use those bonus points.** Repeat after us, "Book clubs are our friends!" At the beginning of each school year, in an effort to entice your loyalty, Scholastic, Troll, and Carnival offer huge rewards for purchasing books from them. This year, Scholastic offered 20 times the bonus points on orders of $200 or more. One school we know used its entire book budget to purchase $200 worth of books and, as a result, received 4,000 bonus points to get more books for free.

- **Shop at yard sales.** Some people are uncomfortable with using secondhand materials. Think of it this way, though: After it has been in your class for ten minutes, it's secondhand. Let someone else pay the depreciation on those expensive hardcover books! Pick them up for pennies at a yard sale. Of course, keep in mind issues of quality. A low-cost or free book of poor quality is truly not worth much. (See chapter 7 for more information about book selection.) Make sure the material is worthy of the time spent reading it. Many books for children—especially those sold at supermarkets or dollar stores, or those based on TV or movie characters—are poorly written. As a rule of thumb, look for books by well-respected authors or that have received noteworthy awards.

- **Make your own materials.** The next time you're heading out to the teacher-supply store, stop and think about how you might save money by using resources that surround you. Instead of buying expensive chart paper, for example, use the backs of advertising posters you can get for free, such as those from bottling plants, for writing class stories, charting out poems or songs, or creating lists of vocabulary words that children associate with the theme.

  Class books are generally easy and inexpensive to make and are often the most selected books in a classroom. Similarly, you can make audiobooks with a printed book, a short blank cassette, and a tape recorder. Use a bell or other tone to indicate when pages should be turned.

- **Ask families to donate materials to the program instead of buying you a holiday gift.** Gift certificates to retail stores or bookstores can go a long way.

- **Ask a civic group like the Rotary Club to sponsor literacy in your program.** Some groups, such as Civitan and Kiwanis, have specific charity goals for their chapters. See if your needs fit with your local chapter's goals.

- **Use your library.** Borrow books from the library for use in your classroom. If you call ahead, many librarians will put together a set of books on a particular topic and/or for a particular age group.

- **Think "Can do!" instead of "Poor me!"** Use underfunding as an opportunity to stretch your creative muscle. Think about what you need—books, paper, writing instruments—and who has it. Ask yourself, "If I can't get precisely what I want, what could be substituted?" and "Who do I know who might help?" You are resourceful and smart. If you can get a 3-year-old to eat peas, you can solve this!

Q I'm afraid if I send books home, they won't come back. What can I do?

A Books might not be returned. To us, though, that's a good thing. It means there is a book in a home that might not otherwise have it. However, your program may be so stretched for resources that too many unreturned books could blow a major hole in your library. Part of the solution is to create reverence for literacy and books among children and families. Talk with families about how important the books are to the classroom. Talk with children about how special books are and how you want them and their friends to have an opportunity to take books home—and how that might not happen if they don't bring them back. Allow only one book out at a time per child. When that one comes back, he or she can take out another. If you create a climate of respect and expect your children and families to abide by it, you may be surprised at how many of those books remain in the library.

Having a large enough collection that losing a book won't be a hardship is another part of the solution. Flesh out your collection by trying some of the suggestions on page 134.

Q I run a small day-care program in my home. Does all this stuff really apply to me?

A Yes. In fact, a number of the photos and ideas in this book come from family day-care homes in Michigan that enroll only up to 12 children. All children are developing literacy understandings, regardless of the setting. We can support those understandings by providing a literacy-rich environment. Just as children come from homes with varying levels of literacy support, family day-care homes can offer varying levels of support. Enrich your home and not only will your own family benefit, but the children in your care will, too.

Q I work with infants. Shouldn't I be spending almost all of my time just snuggling with them? They are too little to be thinking about literacy, aren't they?

A No... and yes. We agree that snuggling babies is a wonderful way to spend your time. We also know that singing to them, talking with them, and, yes, reading to them are as well. When you do these things, babies learn language, become curious about books, and associate the cadence of reading with love and support. We are not asking you to put down the baby... just pick up a book, too!

References

Professional References Cited

Acredolo, L. P., & Goodwyn, S. (1996). *Baby signs: How to talk with your baby before your baby can talk.* Chicago: Contemporary Books.

Adams, M. J. (1990). *Beginning to read: Thinking and learning about print.* Cambridge, MA: MIT Press.

Aiex, N. K. (2005). *Eric digest: Bibliotherapy.* ERIC Clearinghouse on Reading, English, and Communication Digest No. 82. Retrieved May 18, 2005, from http://reading.indiana.edu/ieo/digests/d82.html

Anderson, E., & Guthrie, J. T. (1999, April). *Motivating children to gain conceptual knowledge from text: The combination of science observation and interesting texts.* Paper presented at the annual meeting of the American Educational Research Association, Montreal, Quebec, Canada.

Anderson, R. C., Hiebert, E. H., Scott, J. A., & Wilkinson, L. (1985). *Becoming a nation of readers: The report of the Commission on Reading.* Washington, DC: The National Institute of Education.

Anderson, R. C., & Pearson, P. D. (1984). *A schema-theoretic view of basic processes in reading comprehension* (Tech. Rep. No. 36). Cambridge, MA: Bolt, Beranek and Newman.

Anthony, J. L., Lonigan, C. J., Driscoll, K., Phillips, B. M., & Burgess, S. R. (2002). Phonological sensitivity: A quasi-parallel progression of word structure units and cognitive operations. *Reading Research Quarterly, 38,* 470-487.

Baghban, M. (1984). *Our daughter learns to read and write.* Newark, DE: International Reading Association.

Barnett, W. S. (2001). Preschool education for economically disadvantaged children: Effects on reading achievement and related outcomes. In S. B. Neuman & D. K. Dickinson (Eds.), *Handbook of early literacy research* (pp. 421-443). New York: Guilford Press.

Beals, D. E. (2001). Eating and reading: Links between family conversations with preschoolers and later language and literacy. In D. K. Dickinson & P. O. Tabors (Eds.), *Beginning literacy with language: Young children learning at home and school* (pp. 75-92). Baltimore: Paul H. Brookes.

Beals, D. E., & Snow, C. E. (1994). "Thunder is when the angels are upstairs bowling": Narratives and explanations at the dinner table. *Journal of Narrative and Life History, 4,* 331-352.

Beck, I. L., & McKeown, M. G. (2001). Text talk: Capturing the benefits of read-aloud experiences for young children. *Reading Teacher, 55,* 10-20.

Beck, I. L., McKeown, M. G., & Kucan, L. (2002). *Bringing words to life: Robust vocabulary instruction.* New York: Guilford Press.

Beck, I. L., McKeown, M. G., & Kucan, L. (2003). Taking delight in words: Using oral language to build young children's vocabularies. *American Educator, 27,* 36-39, 41, 45-46.

Bialystok, E. (2001). Metalinguistic aspects of bilingual processing. *Annual Review of Applied Linguistics, 21,* 169-181.

Bissex, G. (1980). *GNYS at work: A child learns to write and read.* Cambridge, MA: Harvard University Press.

Bloodgood, J. W. (1999). What's in a name? Children's name writing and literacy acquisition. *Reading Research Quarterly, 34,* 342-367.

Bodrova, E., & Leong, D. J. (1998). Scaffolding emergent writing in the zone of proximal development. *Literacy Teaching and Learning, 3,* 1-18.

Bornstein, M. H. (Ed.). (1989). *Maternal responsiveness: Characteristics and consequences.* San Francisco: Jossey-Bass.

Burns, M. S., Griffin, P., & Snow, C. E. (Eds.). (1999). *Starting out right: A guide to promoting children's reading success.* Washington, DC: National Academy Press.

Bus, A. G., Van IJzendoorn, M. H., & Pellegrini, A. D. (1995). Joint bookreading makes for success in learning to read: A meta-analysis on intergenerational transmission of literacy. *Review of Educational Research, 65,* 1-21.

Campbell, F. A., Ramey, C. T., Pungello, E., Sparling, J., & Miller-Johnson, S. (2002). Early childhood education: Young adult outcomes from the Abecedarian project. *Applied Developmental Science, 6,* 42-57.

Cazden, C. B. (1969). Suggestions from studies of early language acquisition. *Childhood Education, 46,* 127-131.

Cazden, C. B. (1988). *Classroom discourse: The language of teaching and learning.* Portsmouth, NH: Heinemann.

Clay, M. M. (1966). *Emergent reading behaviour.* Unpublished doctoral dissertation, University of Auckland, Auckland, New Zealand.

Clay, M. M. (1972). *Reading: The patterning of complex behaviour.* Auckland, New Zealand: Heinemann.

Clay, M. M. (1975). *What did I write?* Portsmouth, NH: Heinemann.

Clay, M. M. (1993). *An observation survey of early literacy achievement.* Portsmouth, NH: Heinemann.

Clements, D. H. (1994). The uniqueness of the computer

as a learning tool: Insights from research and practice. In J. Wright & D. Shade (Eds.), *Young children: Active learners in a technological age* (pp. 31–50). Washington, DC: NAEYC.

Clements, D. H., & Nastasi, B. K. (1992). Computers and early childhood education. In M. Gettinger, S. N. Elliott, & T. R. Kratochwill (Eds.), *Advances in school psychology: Preschool and early childhood treatment directions* (pp. 187–246). Hillsdale, NJ: Lawrence Erlbaum Associates.

Cole, M. (1990). Cognitive development and formal schooling: The evidence from cross-cultural research. In L. C. Moll (Ed.), *Vygotsky and education: Instructional implications and applications of sociohistorical psychology* (pp. 89–110). New York: Cambridge University Press.

DeTemple, J. M. (2001). Parents and children reading books together. In D. K. Dickinson & P. O. Tabors (Eds.), *Beginning literacy with language: Young children learning at home and school* (pp. 31–51). Baltimore: Paul H. Brookes.

Dickinson, D. K. (2001a). Large-group and free-play times: Conversational settings and supporting language and literacy development. In D. K. Dickinson & P. O. Tabors (Eds.), *Beginning literacy with language: Young children learning at home and school* (pp. 223–255). Baltimore: Paul H. Brookes.

Dickinson, D. K. (2001b). Putting the pieces together: Impact of preschool on children's language and literacy development in kindergarten. In D. K. Dickinson & P. O. Tabors (Eds.), *Beginning literacy with language: Young children learning at home and school* (pp. 257–287). Baltimore: Paul H. Brookes.

Dickinson, D. K., & Smith, M. W. (1994). Long-term effects of preschool teachers' book readings on low-income children's vocabulary and story comprehension. *Reading Research Quarterly, 29*, 104–122.

Dickinson, D. K., & Sprague, K. E. (2001). The nature and impact of early childhood care environments on the language and early literacy development of children from low-income families. In S. B. Neuman & D. K. Dickinson (Eds.), *Handbook of early literacy research* (pp. 263–280). New York: Guilford Press.

Duke, N. K., & Bennett-Armistead, V. S. (2003). *Reading and writing informational text in the primary grades: Research-based practices.* New York: Scholastic.

Duke, N. K., Moses, A. M., Subedi, D., Billman, A. K., & Zhang, S. (2005). *The frequency and nature of developmentally appropriate emergent literacy activities in child care.* Unpublished manuscript. Michigan State University, East Lansing.

Duke, N. K., & Pearson, P. D. (2002). Effective practices for developing reading comprehension. In A. E. Farstrup & S. J. Samuels (Eds.), *What research has to say about reading instruction* (3rd ed., pp. 205–242). Newark, DE: International Reading Association.

Dunn, L., Beach, S. A., & Kontos, S. (1994). Quality of the literacy environment in daycare and children's development. *Journal of Research in Childhood Education, 9*, 24–34.

Durkin, D. (1966). *Children who read early: Two longitudinal studies.* New York: Teachers College Press.

Dyson, A. H. (1985). Individual differences in emerging writing. In M. Farr (ed.), *Advances in writing research: Vol. 1. Children's early writing development.* Norwood, NJ: Ablex.

Dyson, A. H. (2001). Writing and children's symbolic repertoires: Development unhinged. In S. B. Neuman & D. Dickinson (Eds.), *Handbook of early literacy research* (pp. 126–141). New York: Guilford Press.

Edwards, P. (2004). *Children's literacy development: Making it happen through school, family, and community involvement.* Boston: Allyn and Bacon.

Ehri, L. C. (1989). Movement into word reading and spelling: How spelling contributes to reading. In J. M. Mason (Ed.), *Reading and writing connections* (pp. 65–81). Boston: Allyn and Bacon.

Ehri, L. C., Nunes, S. R., Willows, D. M., Schuster, B. V., Yaghoub-Zadeh, Z., & Shanahan, T. (2001). Phonemic awareness instruction helps children learn to read: Evidence from the national reading panel's meta-analysis. *Reading Research Quarterly, 36*, 250–287.

Ferreiro, E., & Teberosky, A. (1982). *Literacy before schooling.* Portsmouth, NH: Heinemann.

Fox, B. J., & Hull, M. A. (2002). *Phonics for the teacher of reading* (8th ed.). Upper Saddle River, NJ: Prentice Hall.

Garvey, C., & Berndt, C. (1977). Organization of pretend play. *JSAS Catalog of Selected Documents in Psychology: 1* (Ms. No. 1589).

Gates, A. I. (1937). The necessary mental age for beginning reading. *Elementary School Journal, vol. 37,* 497–498.

Gentry, J. R. (1978). Early spelling strategies. *Elementary School Journal, 79*, 88–92.

Girolametto, L., & Weitzman, E. (2002). Responsiveness of child care providers in interactions with toddlers and preschoolers. *Language, Speech, & Hearing Services in Schools, 33*, 268–281.

Goodwyn, S. W., & Acredolo, L. P. (1998). Encouraging symbolic gestures: A new perspective on the relationship between gesture and speech. In J. M. Iverson & S. Goldin-Meadow (Eds.), *The nature and functions of gesture in children's communication* (pp. 61-73). San Francisco: Jossey-Bass.

Goodwyn, S. W., Acredolo, L. P., & Brown, C. A. (2000). Impact of symbolic gesturing on early language development. *Journal of Nonverbal Behavior, 24*, 81-103.

Graves, M. F., & Watts-Taffe, S. M. (2002). The place of word consciousness in a research-based vocabulary program. In A. E. Farstrup and S. J. Samuels (Eds.), *What research has to say about reading instruction* (3rd ed., pp. 140–165). Newark, DE: International Reading Association.

Gray, S. W., Ramsey, B. K., & Klaus, R. A. (1982). *From 3 to 20: The early training project.* Baltimore: University Park Press.

Guthrie, J. (2004). Teaching for literacy engagement. *Journal of Literacy Research, 36*, 2-30.

Harste, J. C., Woodward, V. A., & Burke, C. L. (1984). *Language stories & literacy lessons.* Portsmouth, NH: Heinemann.

Hart, B., & Risley, T. R. (1995). *Meaningful differences in the everyday experience of young American children.* Baltimore: Paul H. Brookes.

Haugland, S. W., & Wright, J. L. (1997). *Young children and technology: A world of discovery.* Boston: Allyn and Bacon.

Howes, C., & Hamilton, C. E. (1992). Children's relationships with caregivers: Mothers and child care teachers. *Child Development, 63*, 859-866.

International Reading Association (IRA) & National Association for the Education of Young Children (NAEYC) (adopted, 1998). *Learning to read and write:*

Developmentally appropriate practices for young children [a joint position statement]. Newark, DE and Washington, DC: Author.

International Reading Association (2005, January). *Literacy development in the preschool years: A position statement of the International Reading Association* [Brochure]. Newark, DE: Author.

Jordan, G. E., Snow, C. E., & Porche, M. V. (2000). Project EASE: The effect of a family literacy project on kindergarten students' early literacy skills. *Reading Research Quarterly, 35*, 524–546.

Katz, J. R. (2001). Playing at home: The talk of pretend play. In D. K. Dickinson & P. O. Tabors (Eds.), *Beginning literacy with language: Young children learning at home and school* (pp. 53-73). Baltimore: Paul H. Brookes.

Kellogg, R. (1969). *Analyzing children's art.* Palo Alto, CA: Mayfield.

Kilmer, S. J., & Hofman, H. (1995). Transforming science curriculum. In S. Bredekamp & T. Rosegrant (Eds.), *Reading potentials: Transforming each childhood curriculum and assessment, vol. 2* (pp. 43-63). Washington, DC: National Association for the Education of Young Children.

Kostelnik, M. J., Whiren A. P., & Stein, L. C. (1986). Living with he-man: Managing superhero fantasy play. *Young children, 41*(4), 3-9.

Kucer, S. B. (2001). *Dimension of literacy: A conceptual base for teaching reading and writing in school settings.* Mahwah, NJ: Lawrence Erlbaum Associates.

Landry, S. H., Smith, K. E., Miller-Loncar, C. L., & Swank, P. R. (1997). Predicting cognitive-language and social growth curves from early maternal behaviors in children at varying degrees of biological risk. *Developmental Psychology, 33*, 1040-1053.

Lee, J. H., & Huston, A. C. (2003). Educational televisual media effect. In E. L. Palmer & B. M. Young (Eds.), *The faces of televisual media: Teaching, violence, selling to children* (pp. 83-106). Mahwah, NJ: Lawrence Erlbaum Associates.

Lightfoot-Lawrence, S. (2004). *The essential conversation: What parents and teachers can learn from each other.* New York: Random House.

Lowenfeld, V. (1954). *Your child and his art: A guide for parents.* New York: Macmillan.

MacDonald, S. (1997). *The portfolio and its use: A road map for assessment.* Little Rock, AR: Southern Early Childhood Association.

Malchiodi, C. A. (1998). *Understanding children's drawing.* New York: Guilford Press.

McCartney, K. (1984). Effect of quality of daycare environment on children's language development. *Developmental Psychology, 20*, 224-260.

McGee, L., Lomax, R., & Head, M. (1988). Young children's written language knowledge: What environmental and functional print reading reveals. *Journal of Reading Behavior, 20*, 99-118.

McGill-Franzen, A., Allington, R. L., Yokoi, L., & Brooks, G. (1999). Putting books in the classroom seems necessary but not sufficient. *Journal of Educational Research, 93*, 67-74.

McGuinness, D. (1997). *Why our children can't read and what we can do about it: A scientific revolution in reading.* New York: Free Press.

McKeown, M. G., & Beck, I. L. (2003). Taking advantage of read alouds to help children make sense of decontextualized language. In A. van Kleeck, S. A. Stahl, and E. B. Bauer (Eds.), *On reading books to children: Parents and teachers* (pp. 159-176). Mahwah, NJ: Lawrence Erlbaum Associates.

Mehan, H. (1979). *Learning lessons: Social organization in the classroom.* Cambridge, MA: Harvard University Press.

Moll, L. (1992). Funds of knowledge for teaching: Using a qualitative approach to connect homes and classrooms. *Theory into Practice, 31*, 132-141.

Morphett, M. V., & Washburne, C. (1931). When should children begin to read? *Elementary School Journal, 31*, 496-501.

Morrow, L. M. (1985). Retelling stories: A strategy for improving young children's comprehension, concept of story structure, and oral language complexity. *Elementary School Journal, 85*, 647-661.

Morrow, L. M. (1989). *Literacy development in the early years: Helping children learn to read and write.* Boston: Allyn and Bacon.

Morrow, L. M. (1990). Preparing the classroom environment to promote literacy during play. *Early Childhood Research Quarterly, 5*, 537-554.

Morrow, L. M. (1993). *Literacy development in the early years: Helping children learn to read and write* (2nd ed.). Boston, MA: Allyn and Bacon.

Morrow, L. M. (2002). *The literacy center: Contexts for reading and writing* (2nd ed.). Portland, ME: Stenhouse.

Morrow, L. M., & Weinstein, C. S. (1986). Encouraging voluntary reading: The impact of a literature program on children's use of library centers. *Reading Research Quarterly, 21*, 330-346.

National Association for the Education of Young Children (NAEYC). (1996). *Technology and young children—ages 3 through 8: A position statement of the National Association for the Education of Young Children.* Washington, DC: Author.

National Association for the Education of Young Children. (1997). *Developmentally appropriate practice in early childhood programs serving children from birth through 8.* Washington, DC: Author.

National Center for Improving Science Education. (1990). *Getting started in science: A blueprint for elementary school education. A report from the National Center for Improving Science Education.* Colorado Springs, CO: Author.

Neuman, S. B. (1996). Children engaging in storybook reading: The influence of access to print resources, opportunity and parental interaction. *Early Childhood Research Quarterly, 11*, 495-514.

Neuman, S. B. (1999). Books make a difference: A study of access to literacy. *Reading Research Quarterly, 34*, 286-311.

Neuman, S. B., Celano, D. C., Greco, A. N., & Shue, P. (2001). *Access for all: Closing the book gap for children in early education.* Newark, DE: International Reading Association.

Neuman, S. B., Copple, C., & Bredekamp, S. (2000). *Learning to read and write: Developmentally appropriate practices for young children.* Washington, DC: National Association for the Education of Young Children.

Neuman, S. B., & Roskos, K. (1989). Preschoolers' conceptions of literacy as reflected in their spontaneous play. In S. McCormick & J. Zutell (Eds.), *Cognitive and social perspectives for literacy research and instruction* (pp. 87-94). Chicago: National Reading Conference.

Neuman, S. B., & Roskos, K. (1993a). *Language and literacy learning in the early years: An integrated approach.* Fort Worth, TX: Harcourt Brace Jovanovich.

Neuman, S. B., & Roskos, K. (1993b). Access to print for children of poverty: Differential effects of adult mediation and literacy-enriched play settings on environmental and functional print tasks. *American Educational Research Journal, 30*, 95-122.

No Child Left Behind Act of 2001, Pub. L. No. 107-110, §§ 1221-1226, 115 Stat. 1425, 1552-1555 (2002).

Nystrand, M., Gamoran, A., Kachur, R., & Prendergast, C. (1997). *Opening dialogue: Understanding the dynamics of language and learning in the English classroom.* New York: Teachers College Press.

Orellana, M. F., & Hernández, A. (1999). Taking the walk: Children reading urban environmental print. *The Reading Teacher, 52*, 612-619.

Palincsar, A. S., & Magnusson, S. J. (2000). *The interplay of firsthand and text-based investigations in science education.* Ann Arbor: Center for the Improvement of Early Reading Achievement, University of Michigan.

Purcell-Gates, V. (1988). Lexical and syntactic knowledge of written narrative held by well-read-to kindergartners and second graders. *Research in the Teaching of English, 22*, 128-160.

Purcell-Gates, V. (1996). Stories, coupons, and the TV Guide: Relationships between home literacy experiences and emergent literacy knowledge. *Reading Research Quarterly, 31*, 406-428.

Purcell-Gates, V., McIntyre, E., & Freppon, P. A. (1995). Learning written storybook language in school: A comparison of low-SES children in skills-based and whole language classrooms. *American Educational Research Journal, 32*, 659-685.

Richgels, D. J. (2001). Invented spelling, phonemic awareness, and reading and writing instruction. In S. B. Neuman & D. K. Dickinson (Eds.), *Handbook of early literacy research* (pp. 142-155). New York: Guilford Press.

Roberts, E. M. (2003). Professional discussions and development: Exploring informational text in study groups and other activities with colleagues. In N. K. Duke, & V. S. Bennett-Armistead, with A. Huxley, M. K. Johnson, D. McLurkin, E. M. Roberts, C. Rosen, & E. Vogel (Eds.), *Reading and writing informational text in the primary grades: Research-based practices.* (pp. 229-238). New York: Scholastic.

Rogoff, B., & Chavajay, P. (1995). What's become of research on the cultural basis of cognitive development? *American Psychologist, 50,* 859-877.

Roskos, K., and Christie, J. (2001). Examining the play-literacy interface: A critical review and future directions. *Journal of Early Childhood Literacy, 1,* 59-89.

Roskos, K., & Neuman, S. B. (2001). Environment and its influences for early literacy teaching and learning. In S. B. Neuman & D. K. Dickinson (Eds.), *Handbook of early literacy research* (pp. 281-292). New York: Guilford Press.

Saunders, W. M., & Goldenberg, C. (1999). Effects of instructional conversations and literature logs on limited- and fluent- English proficient students' story comprehension and thematic understanding. *The Elementary School Journal, 99,* 277-301.

Scarborough, H. S. (2001). Connecting early language and literacy to later reading (dis)abilities: Evidence, theory, and practice. In S. B. Neuman & D. K. Dickinson (Eds.), *Handbook of early literacy research* (pp. 97-110). New York: Guilford Press.

Schweinhart, L. J., Barnes, H. V., & Weikart, D. P. (1993). *Significant benefits: The High/Scope Perry preschool study through age 27.* (Monographs of the High/Scope Educational Research Foundation No. 10). Ypsilanti, MI: High/Scope Educational Research Foundation.

Senechal, M., & LeFevre, J. (2002). Parental involvement in the development of children's reading skill: A five-year longitudinal study. *Child Development, 73,* 445-460.

Shanahan, T., Lonigan. C. J., Strickland, D. S., & Westburg, L. (2004, May). *The National Early Literacy Panel: A synthesis of what the research has to say about young children's literacy development.* Presentation at Reading Research 2004: Moving Forward on Many Fronts, Reno, NV.

Sinclair, J. M., & Coulthard, M. (1975). *Towards an analysis of discourse: The English used by teachers and pupils.* London: Oxford University Press.

Smith, M. C. (2000). The real-world reading practices of adults. *Journal of Literacy Research, 32,* 25-52.

Snow, C. E. (1983). Literacy and language: Relationships during the preschool years. *Harvard Educational Review, 53*(2), 165-189.

Snow, C. E., Burns, M. S., & Griffin, P. (Eds.). (1998). *Preventing reading difficulties in young children.* Washington, DC: National Academy Press.

Soderman, A. K., Gregory, K. M., & McCarty, L. T. (2005). *Scaffolding emergent literacy: A child-centered approach for preschool through grade 5* (2nd ed.). Boston: Allyn and Bacon.

Soderman, A. K., Gregory, K. M., & O'Neill, L. T. (1999). *Scaffolding emergent literacy: A child-centered approach for preschool through grade 5.* Boston: Allyn and Bacon.

Stanovich, K. E. (1986). Matthew effects in reading: Some consequences of individual differences in the acquisition of literacy. *Reading Research Quarterly, 21,* 360-407.

Sulzby, E. (1985a). Kindergarteners as writers and readers. In M. Farr (Ed.), *Advances in writing research: Vol. 1. Children's early writing.* Norwood, NJ: Ablex.

Sulzby, E. (1985b). Children's emergent reading of favorite storybooks: A developmental study. *Reading Research Quarterly, 20,* 458-481.

Sulzby, E. (1986). Writing and reading: Signs of oral and written language organization in the young child. In W. H. Teale & E. Sulzby (Eds.), *Emergent literacy: Writing and reading* (pp. 50-89). Norwood, NJ: Ablex.

Tabors, P. O., Beals, D. E., & Weizman, Z. O. (2001). "You know what oxygen is?" Learning new words at home. In D. K. Dickinson & P. O. Tabors (Eds.), *Beginning literacy with language: Young children learning at home and school* (pp. 93-110). Baltimore: Paul H. Brookes.

Tamis-LeMonda, C. S., Bornstein, M. H., & Baumwell, L. (2001). Maternal responsiveness and children's achievement of language milestones. *Child Development, 72,* 748-767.

Taylor, D., & Dorsey-Gaines, C. (1988). *Growing up literate: Learning from inner-city families.* Portsmouth, NH: Heinemann.

Teale, W. H., & Sulzby, E. (Eds.). (1986a). *Emergent literacy: Writing and reading.* Norwood, NJ: Ablex.

Teale, W. H., & Sulzby, E. (1986b). Introduction: Emergent literacy. In W. H. Teale & E. Sulzby (Eds.), *Emergent literacy: Writing and reading* (pp. vii–xxv). Norwood, NJ: Ablex.

Tharp, R. (1982). The effective instruction of comprehension: Results and description of the Kamehameha Early Education Program. *Reading Research Quarterly, 17,* 503–527.

Thompson, C. M. (1995). Transforming curriculum in the visual arts. In S. Bredekamp & T. Rosegrant (Eds.), *Reading potentials: Transforming each childhood curriculum and assessment* (Vol. 2, pp. 81–98). Washington, DC: National Association for the Education of Young Children.

Van Kleeck, A., Stahl, S. A., & Bauer, E. B. (Eds.). (2003). *On reading books to children: Parents and teachers.* Mahwah, NJ: Lawrence Erlbaum Associates.

Venezky, R. L. (1999). *The American way of spelling: The structure and origins of American English orthography.* New York: Guilford Press.

Vivas, E. (1996). Effects of story reading on language. *Language Learning, 46,* 189–216.

Whitehurst, G. J., Arnold, D. S., Epstein, J. N., Angell, A. L., Smith, M., & Fischel, J. E. (1994). A picture book reading intervention in daycare and home for children from low-income families. *Developmental Psychology, 30,* 679–689.

Whitehurst, G. J., Epstein, J. N., Angell, A. L., Payne, A. C., Crone, D. A., & Fischel, J. E. (1994). Outcomes of an emergent literacy intervention in Head Start. *Journal of Educational Psychology, 86,* 542–555.

Whitehurst, G. J., & Lonigan, C. J. (2001). Emergent literacy: Development from prereaders to readers. In S. B. Neuman & D. K. Dickinson (Eds.), *Handbook of early literacy research* (pp. 11–29). New York: Guilford Press.

Wilson, P. T., & Anderson, R. C. (1986). What they don't know will hurt them: The role of prior knowledge in comprehension. In J. Oransano (Ed.), *Reading comprehension from research to practice* (pp. 31–48). Hillsdale, NJ: Lawrence Erlbaum Associates.

Wood, J. M. (2004). *Literacy online: New tools for struggling readers and writers.* Portsmouth, NH: Heinemann.

Worth, K., & Grollman, S. (2003). *Worms, shadows, and whirlpools: Science in the early childhood classroom.* Portsmouth, NH: Heinemann.

Zevenbergen, A. A., & Whitehurst, G. J. (2003). Dialogic reading: A shared picture book reading intervention for preschoolers. In A. van Kleeck, S. A. Stahl, & E. B. Bauer (Eds.), *On reading Books to children: parents and teachers* (pp. 177–200). Mahwah, NJ: Lawrence Erlbaum Associates.

Children's Books Cited

Ahlberg, A. (1986). *The jolly postman.* Illustrated by J. Ahlberg. Boston: Little, Brown.

Ahlberg, A. (1991). *The jolly Christmas postman.* Illustrated by J. Ahlberg. Boston: Little, Brown.

Alborough, J. (1994). *It's the bear!* Cambridge, MA: Candlewick Press.

Alborough, J. (2000). *Duck in the truck.* New York: HarperCollins.

Awan, S. (2000). *My first farm board book.* New York: Dorling Kindersley.

Barton, B. (1989). *Dinosaurs, dinosaurs.* New York: HarperCollins Publishers.

Barton, B. (1993). *The little red hen.* New York: HarperFestival.

Barton, B. (1997). *Machines at work.* New York: HarperFestival.

Barton, B. (2001). *My car.* New York: Greenwillow Books.

Bemelmans, L. (1939). *Madeline.* New York: Puffin.

Bond, F. (1996). *Tumble bumble.* New York: HarperCollins.

Bourgeois, P. (2000). *Garbage collectors.* Illustrated by K. Lafave. New York: Kids Can Press.

Boynton, S. (1977). *Hippos go berserk!* New York: Simon & Schuster.

Boynton, S. (1984). *Blue hat, green hat.* New York: Simon & Schuster.

Bradley, K. B. (2001). *Pop! A book about bubbles.* Photographs by M. Miller. New York: HarperTrophy.

Brown, M. W. (1942). *The runaway bunny.* Illustrated by C. Hurd. New York: HarperFestival.

Brown, M. W. (1994). *Big red barn.* Illustrated by F. Bond. New York: HarperFestival.

Bunting, E. (2002). *Girls a to z.* Illustrated by S. Bloom. Honesdale, PA: Boyd Mills Press.

Burris, P. (2003). *Five green and speckled frogs.* New York: Cartwheel.

Campbell, R. (1986). *Dear zoo*. New York: Little Simon.

Canizares, S., & Chanko, P. (1999). *Signs*. New York: Scholastic.

Carle, E. (1984). *The very busy spider*. New York: Philomel Books.

Carle, E. (1994). *The very hungry caterpillar*. New York: Philomel Books.

Carle, E. (1999). *From head to toe*. New York: HarperFestival.

Carter, D. (2002). *Get to work trucks!* Brookfield, CT: Roaring Brook Press.

Christelow, E. (1989). *Five little monkeys jumping on the bed*. New York: Scholastic.

Cole, J., & Calmenson, S. (1993). *Six sick sheep: 101 tongue twisters*. Illustrated by A. Tiegreen. New York: HarperCollins.

Cooper, K. (1995). *Too many rabbits and other fingerplays about animals, nature, weather, and the universe*. Illustrated by Judith Moffatt. New York: Scholastic.

Crews, D. (1978). *Freight train*. New York: Greenwillow Books.

Crews, N. (2004). *The neighborhood Mother Goose*. New York: Greenwillow Books.

Crosbie, M. J., & Rosenthal, S. (1995). *Architecture animals*. Hoboken, NJ: John Wiley & Sons.

Crosbie, M. J., & Rosenthal, S. (1995). *Architecture counts*. Hoboken, NJ: John Wiley & Sons.

Crosbie, M. J., & Rosenthal, S. (1995). *Architecture shapes*. Hoboken, NJ: John Wiley & Sons.

De Brunoff, L. (2003). *Babar's museum of art*. New York: Harry N. Abrams.

Degen, B. (1994). *Jamberry*. New York: HarperFestival.

Delafosse, C. & Gallimard, J. (1999). *Under the sea*. Illustrated by P. De Hugo. New York: Scholastic.

Demarest, C. L. (1988). *No peas for Nellie*. New York: Simon & Schuster.

Demarest, C. L. (2000). *Firefighters from a to z*. New York: Scholastic.

DePaola, T. (1985). *Tomie's little Mother Goose*. New York: G. P. Putnam and Sons.

Dodds, D. A. (1996). *The shape of things*. Illustrated by J. Lacome. Cambridge, MA: Candlewick Press.

Donaldson, J. (2001). *Room on the broom*. Illustrated by A. Scheffler. New York: Scholastic.

Dorling Kindersley. (1994). *The big book of things that go*. New York: Author.

Dorling Kindersley. (1997). *My first word board book*. New York: Author.

Dorling Kindersley. (1998). *Baby faces*. New York: Author.

Dorling Kindersley. (1998). *My first a b c board book*. New York: Author.

Dorling Kindersley. (1998). *Touch and feel: Clothes*. New York: Author.

Dorling Kindersley. (1998). *Touch and feel: Farm*. New York: Author.

Dorling Kindersley. (2000). *Touch and feel: Shapes*. New York: Author.

Dorling Kindersley. (2001). *Baseball a b c*. New York: Author.

Dorling Kindersley. (2003). *Are lemons blue?* New York: Author.

Dorling Kindersley. (2003). *Cats*. New York: Author.

Dorling Kindersley. (2005). *Dogs*. New York: Author.

Dr. Seuss. (1963). *Hop on pop*. New York: Random House.

Dr. Seuss. (1970). *Mr. Brown can moo! Can you? Dr. Seuss's book of wonderful noises*. New York: Random House.

Dr. Seuss. (1974). *There's a wocket in my pocket*. New York: Random House.

Ehlert, L. (1997). *Color zoo*. New York: HarperCollins.

Ehlert, L. (1999). *Snowballs*. New York: Voyager Books.

Emberley, E. (2000). *My colors, mis colores*. New York: Little, Brown.

Emberley, E. (2001). *A wing on a flea: A book about shapes*. New York: Little, Brown.

Falwell, C. (1993). *Feast for 10*. New York: Clarion Books.

Father Gander. (1986). *Father Gander's nursery rhymes: The equal rhymes amendment*. Santa Barbara, CA: Advocacy Press.

Flanagan, A. (1999). *Officer Brown keeps neighborhoods safe*. Photographs by C. Osinski. New York: Children's Press.

Fleming, D. (2002). *Alphabet under construction*. New York: Henry Holt and Company.

Folsom, M. M., & Elting, M. (1985). *Q is for duck: An alphabet guessing game*. Illustrated by J. K. Kent. New York: Clarion Books.

Foote, B. J. (2001). *Cup cooking: Individual child portion picture recipes*. New York: Gryphon House.

Freeman, D. (1968). *Corduroy*. New York: Puffin.

Galdone, P. (1972). *The three bears*. New York: Clarion Books.

Galdone, P. (1981). *Three billy goats gruff*. New York: Clarion Books.

George, L. B. (1995). *In the woods: Who's been here?* New York: Greenwillow Books.

Gibbons, G. (1982). *The post office book: Mail and how it moves*. New York: HarperCollins.

Gibbons, G. (1987). *Fire! Fire!* New York: HarperTrophy.

Gibbons, G. (2000). *Apples*. New York: Holiday House.

Goodall, J. S. (1975). *Creepy castle*. New York: Simon & Schuster.

Guarino, D. (1989). *Is your mama a llama?* Illustrated by S. Kellogg. New York: Scholastic.

Hague, M. (1993). *Teddy bear, teddy bear: A classic action rhyme.* New York: Morrow Junior Books

Hindley, J. (1999). *Eyes, nose, fingers, and toes.* Cambridge, MA: Candlewick Press.

Hoban, T. (1983). *I read signs.* New York: Scholastic.

Hoban, T. (1983). *I read symbols.* New York: Greenwillow Books.

Hoban, T. (1985). *A children's zoo.* New York: Greenwillow Books.

Hoban, T. (1999). *Construction zone.* New York: Greenwillow Books.

Hoberman, M.A. (1998). *Miss Mary Mack.* Illustrated by N.B. Wescott. Boston: Little, Brown.

Hoberman, M. A. (2000). *The seven silly eaters.* Illustrated by M. Frazee. Orlando, FL: Voyager Books.

Hutchings, A. (1994). *Picking apples and pumpkins.* New York: Scholastic.

Ingle, A. (1992). *Zoo animals.* New York: Random House.

Intrater, R. G. (1997). *Peek-a-boo!* New York: Scholastic.

Intrater, R. G. (2000). *Two eyes, a nose, and a mouth.* New York: Scholastic.

J. Paul Getty Museum. (1997). *A is for artist: A Getty Museum alphabet.* Los Angeles: Author.

James, S. (1991). *Dear Mr. Blueberry.* New York: Macmillan.

Jenkins, S. (2004). *Actual size.* Boston: Houghton Mifflin.

Jenkins, S., & Page, R. (2003). *What do you do with a tail like this?* Boston: Houghton Mifflin.

Johnson, S. T. (1995). *Alphabet city.* New York: Puffin.

Johnson, S. T. (1998). *City by numbers.* New York: Puffin.

Jonas, A. (1989) *Color dance.* New York: Greenwillow Books.

Katz, K. (2000). *Where is baby's belly button?* New York: Simon & Schuster.

Katzen, M., & Henderson, A. (1994). *Pretend soup and other real recipes: A cookbook for preschoolers & up.* San Francisco: Tricycle Press.

Keats, E. J. (1962). *The snowy day.* New York: Penguin Putnam.

Kirk, D. (2000). *Miss Spider's a b c.* New York: Scholastic.

Kunhardt, D. (1940). *Pat the bunny.* New York: Simon & Schuster.

Laden, N. (2000). *Peek-a-who?* San Francisco: Chronicle Books.

Leeper, A. (2004). *Landfill.* Portsmouth, NH: Heinemann.

Levenson, G. (1999). *Pumpkin circle.* Photographs by S. Thaler. Berkeley, CA: Tricycle Press.

Liebman, D. (2000). *I want to be a police officer.* Buffalo, NY: Firefly Books.

Lionni, L. (1963). *Swimmy.* New York: Scholastic.

Maass, R. (1996). *Fire fighters.* New York: Scholastic.

Marshall, J. (1997). *Goldilocks and the three bears.* New York: Penguin Putnam.

Martin, B., Jr. (1967) *Brown bear, brown bear, what do you see?* Illustrated by E. Carle. New York: Holt, Rinehart and Winston.

Martin, B., Jr., & Archambault, J. (1989). *Chicka chicka boom boom.* Illustrated by L. Ehlert. New York: Simon & Schuster.

Marzollo, J. (1997). *Pretend you're a cat.* Illustrated by J. Pinkney. New York: Puffin.

Mayer, M. (1974). *One monster after another.* Columbus, OH: McGraw-Hill Children's Publishing.

McCloskey, R. (1941). *Make way for ducklings.* New York: Viking.

Metropolitan Museum of Art. (2002). *Museum a b c.* New York: Little, Brown.

Meyers, S. (2004). *Everywhere babies.* Illustrated by M. Frazee. San Diego, CA: Harcourt.

Micklethwait, L. (1992). *I spy: An alphabet in art.* New York: Greenwillow Books.

Milich, Z. (2002). *City signs.* Toronto, Ontario, Canada: Kids Can Press.

Miller, M. (1990). *Who uses this?* New York: Scholastic.

Miller, M. (1997). *Water play.* New York: Simon & Schuster.

Miller, M. (1998). *Baby faces.* New York: Little Simon.

Miller, M. (2000). *Baby food.* New York: Little Simon.

Miller, M. (2004). *Baby talk.* New York: Little Simon.

Numeroff, L. (1998). *If you give a pig a pancake.* Illustrated by F. Bond. New York: HarperCollins.

Palatini, M. (1995). *Piggie pie.* Illustrated by H. Fine. New York: Clarion Books.

Pallotta, J. (1991). *The underwater alphabet book.* Illustrated by E. Stewart. Watertown, MA: Charlesbridge.

Parr, T. (2001). *It's okay to be different.* Boston: Little, Brown.

Parr, T. (2003). *The family book.* Boston: Little, Brown.

Pinkard, N. (2000). Say say oh playmate [Computer software and manual]. Retrieved from http://www.umich.edu/~medal/ssopmweb/ssop.html.

Pinkney, S. L. (2002). *A rainbow all around me.* Photographs by M. C. Pinkney. New York: Scholastic.

Provensen, A., & Provensen, M. (2001). *The year at Maple Hill Farm.* New York: Aladdin Paperbacks.

Raffi. (1987). *Down by the bay.* Illustrated by N. B. Westcott. New York: Crown.

Raffi. (1997). *Baby beluga.* Illustrated by A. Wolff. New York: Crown.

Rathmann, P. (1994). *Good night gorilla.* New York: G. P. Putnam and Sons.

Reid, M. E. (1996). *Let's find out about ice cream.* Photographs by J. Williams. New York: Scholastic.

Ricklem, N. (1991). *Baby outside.* New York: Little Simon.

Robbins, K. (2003). *Autumn leaves.* New York: Scholastic.

Rosen, M. (1989). *We're going on a bear hunt.* Illustrated by H. Oxenbury. New York: Margaret K. McElderry Books.

Rotner, S., & Kreisler, K. (1992). *Nature spy.* Photographs by S. Rotner. New York: Scholastic.

Rovetch, L. (2001). *Ook the book and other silly rhymes.* Illustrated by S. McNeill. San Francisco: Chronicle Books.

Royston, A. (1992). *Insects and crawly creatures.* Photographs by J. Young. New York: Little Simon.

Ryan, P. M. (2001). *Hello ocean.* Illustrated by M. Astrella. New York: Scholastic.

Saltzberg, B. (2000). *Animal kisses.* San Diego, CA: Red Wagon.

Saltzberg, B. (2001). *Baby animal kisses.* San Diego, CA: Red Wagon.

Saltzberg, B. (2002). *Peekaboo kisses.* San Diego, CA: Red Wagon.

Saltzberg, B. (2004). *Noisy kisses.* San Diego, CA: Red Wagon.

Sandved, K. B. (1996). *The butterfly alphabet book.* New York: Scholastic.

Sendak, M. (1963). *Where the wild things are.* New York: Harper & Row.

Shannon, G. (1996). *Tomorrow's alphabet.* Illustrated by D. Crews. New York: Greenwillow Books.

Shaw, N. (1997). *Sheep in a shop.* Illustrated by M. Apple. Boston: Houghton Mifflin.

Shelby, A. (1991). *Potluck.* Illustrated by I. Trivas. New York: Orchard Books.

Showers, P. (1994). *Where does the garbage go?* (Rev. ed.) Illustrated by R. Chewning. New York: HarperCollins.

Shulevitz, U. (1986). *The treasure.* New York: Farrar, Straus & Giroux.

Sill, C. (1991). *About birds: A guide for children.* Illustrated by J. Sill. Atlanta, GA: Peachtree.

Silverstein, S. (2005). *Runny babbit: A billy sook.* New York: HarperCollins.

Simmons, J. (1997). *Come along, Daisy!* New York: Scholastic.

Sloat, T. (2000). *Farmer Brown shears his sheep: A yarn about wool.* Illustrated by N. Wescott. New York: Dorling Kindersley.

Slobodkina, E. (1975). *Caps for sale.* New York: HarperCollins.

Spinelli, E. (1998). *When mama comes home tonight.* Illustrated by J. Dyer. New York: Simon & Schuster Books for Young Readers.

Spinelli, E. (2000). *Night shift daddy.* Illustrated by M. Iwai. New York: Hyperion.

Steptoe, J. (1987). *Mufaro's beautiful daughters.* New York: Amistad.

Stevenson, R. L. (1999). *A child's garden of verses.* Illustrated by T. Tudor. New York: Simon & Schuster Books for Young Readers.

Stillinger, D. (2004). *The Klutz book of paper airplanes.* Palo Alto, CA: Klutz.

Stone, J. (1971). *The monster at the end of this book.* Illustrated by M. Smollin. Racine, WI: Western Publishing Company.

Van Allsburg, C. (1987). *The z was zapped: A play in twenty-six acts.* Boston: Houghton Mifflin.

Van Fleet, M. (1995). *Fuzzy yellow ducklings.* New York: Dial Books for Young Readers.

Voss, G. (1993). *Museum colors: Museum of Fine Arts Boston.* Boston: Museum of Fine Arts.

Voss, G. (1993). *Museum numbers: Museum of Fine Arts Boston.* Boston: Museum of Fine Arts.

Voss, G. (1993). *Museum shapes: Museum of Fine Arts Boston.* Boston: Museum of Fine Arts.

Walsh, M. (1997). *Do monkeys tweet?* Boston: Houghton Mifflin.

Wegman, W. (1994). *ABC.* New York: Hyperion.

Weninger, B., & Moller, A. (2001). *Little apple: A book of thanks.* New York: North-South Books.

Wiesner, D. (1991). *Tuesday.* New York: Clarion Books.

Wilkes, A. (1997). *My first word book.* New York: Dorling Kindersley.

Williams, S. (1996). *I went walking.* Illustrated by J. Vivas. New York: Gulliver Books, Harcourt.

Wood, A. (1992). *Silly Sally.* San Diego, CA: Harcourt.

Wood, A. (1997). *Piggies.* Illustrated by D. Wood. Orlando, FL: Voyager Books.

Wood, A. (1998). *I'm as quick as a cricket.* Illustrated by D. Wood. Swindon, England: Child's Play.

Yee, H. W. (1996). *Fireman small.* Boston: Houghton Mifflin.

Zelinsky, P. O. (1990). *The wheels on the bus.* New York: Penguin Putnam.

Ziefert, H. (2002). *Toes have wiggles kids have giggles.* Illustrated by R. Doughty. New York: G. P. Putnam and Sons.

Index